Starting Out in Project Management

A Study Guide for the APM
Introductory Certificate in Project Management

Second edition

APM Publishing Limited
Ibis House,
Regent Park,
Summerleys Road
Princes Risborough,
Buckinghamshire
HP27 9LE

First published 2004
Second edition 2007
Reprinted 2007, 2008, 2009

British Library Cataloguing in Publication Data is available.

ISBN 10: 1-903494-16-8
ISBN 13: 978-1-903494-16-5

Designed and typeset in 10/12 Optima
by RefineCatch Limited, Bungay, Suffolk
Printed and bound in Great Britain by
CPI Antony Rowe, Chippenham, Wiltshire
Cover design by Hannah Armstrong
Copy editor Merle Read
Proofreader Dorothy Courtis
Publishing Manager Ingmar Folkmans

Starting Out in Project Management

Contents

List of figures

Acknowledgements

We would like to acknowledge the contribution of all those who directly or indirectly have been involved in the development of this manuscript and in the development of the Introductory Certificate in Project Management over the past three years. There are a large number of you, and we cannot list you all here – though Ron Ford of Oxford Projects must be mentioned as he read this manuscript and provided valuable insight from a trainer's perspective. We are particularly indebted to those whose ideas have inspired ours and whose work has contributed to the understanding and application of project management in all sectors of the economy in the United Kingdom and abroad. We have done our best to acknowledge every source and intellectual contribution, but where we have not been able to do so explicitly we do so now.

It was Sue Beavil, former Head of Professional Services at the Association for Project Management, and her work with the UK Government Department for Education and Skills that brought the APM Introductory Certificate in Project Management to fruition. This work officially acknowledged that project management is no longer a subject for a few people in a few business sectors. Since its introduction the new qualification has gone from strength to strength.

The title for this book – *Starting Out in Project Management* – was chosen because, as well as being a comprehensive study guide for anyone wishing to work towards the APM Introductory Certificate in Project Management on a self-taught basis, it is also intended as a good general read and reference book about project management for people who are working in projects but are not project managers. Some people will continue down the road towards professional accreditation in project management. Others will continue with their own profession but with project management as an essential additional skill when faced with bringing about change.

We cannot finish without expressing our thanks to Ingmar Folkmans of APM Publishing for providing us with the opportunity to revise this book and publish the second edition of the 'Study Guide'. We hope that many people will find it very useful and that the generic and simple nature of the text will in some way bring together often disparate views about our profession.

Ruth Murray-Webster
Peter Simon
Meltham and Aylesbury, 2006

Introduction

Starting Out in Project Management has been prepared both as a general introduction to project management and, more specifically, to support students wishing to take the examination for the Association for Project Management's Introductory Certificate in Project Management.

In order for the book to directly support study for the qualification, it is designed to be used in a modular fashion. Students can refer to the APM Introductory Certificate in Project Management syllabus (in Appendix 1) and follow each topic in the sequence presented in the syllabus. They or their tutors can also change that sequence. They can also read the study guide straight through, from the first to the last page.

To support those who prefer to read from start to finish, the chapter order does not follow the order of the detailed syllabus and its specified learning outcomes because this is not the order in which the topics need to be understood and performed when managing a project. The decision to write in this sequence means that the numbering of each chapter does not reflect the numbering system of the syllabus in Appendix 1, but a mapping of chapter numbers to the syllabus is included as Appendix 2.

Please note that the Introductory Certificate in Project Management syllabus at Appendix 1 reflects the structure of the fifth edition of the *APM Body of Knowledge*, which was published in January 2006 and for which examinations commenced in late October 2006. The *APM Body of Knowledge* 5th edition contains 52 topics. The Introductory Certificate in Project Management syllabus contains a subset of these topics, 27 out of 52, as all are not relevant when starting out in project management. For those who were familiar with the version of the Introductory Certificate mapped to the fourth edition of the *Body of Knowledge*, we have included an easy comparison of changes as Appendix 3.

To meet the dual requirements of being a study guide and also a good general guide to project management, on some occasions concepts are included which are slightly more advanced than the Introductory Certificate syllabus requires. The authors have done this to reflect common practice. Where this happens it is noted specifically in the relevant chapter.

Embedded in every chapter is a set of reflective questions to help students to link the theory with their own experience. In addition to the personal reflection, a case study example runs throughout the book and is used to illustrate the learning objectives. APM Publishing would like to thank the charity Comic Relief for allowing the use of its charitable fundraising work and the Red Nose Day brand as a theme for the case study. In recognition of this, APM Publishing will make a donation to Comic Relief for every copy of the book that is sold.

One of the many dilemmas facing those who work on projects or in organisations where project management is practised is the terminology used. Unfortunately there is no globally accepted standard for project management terms. To help the reader in using this book, key terms are either highlighted in **bold italics** and defined in the text, or are in *italics* and marked with an asterisk and defined in a footnote. In addition, a short glossary of official APM terms is included as Appendix 4.

A number of project management terms are used interchangeably throughout this guide, and often with a meaning that differs from the standard dictionary definition. Readers should also be aware that different terms may be used within their particular organisation, although hopefully these instances will not be the norm.

For the purpose of the book a number of terms are used interchangeably. For purists, the authors are not saying that in advanced technical project management language the words necessarily mean the same thing, but for people starting out in project management the synonyms work quite adequately.

Terms used interchangeably are:

- time *and* schedule *and* delivery
- cost *and* budget
- quality *and* performance
- product *and* deliverable
- success criteria *and* objectives
- float *and* slack
- steering group *and* project board
- issue log *and* issue register
- risk log *and* risk register
- change log *and* change register
- procurement *and* purchasing *and* contracting.

Project management 1

Topic 1.1 in the *APM Body of Knowledge* deals with projects and project management as compared to business-as-usual and project management processes. Understanding what is meant by these definitions means that people who are starting out in project management can understand what a project is and separate the activities that make up a project from other routine work that needs to be done.

DEFINE A PROJECT AND THE DIFFERENCES BETWEEN A PROJECT AND BUSINESS-AS-USUAL

At its simplest level the word **project** is used to describe activities that are done to meet specific objectives for change. Changes that are managed as projects can be amendments to things that already exist, or the introduction of new things. A project can involve new products, new services, or improvement to existing products or services. Whatever the cause of the change and the nature of the project, the principles of project management always apply.

Even though project work involves doing new things, it still needs to be controlled, so that the specific objectives are met and the organisation actually gains the desired benefits. One way that this control is achieved is by setting additional objectives or constraints for time, cost and quality. Some people and some organisations prefer to use the term performance rather than quality. The terms are interchangeable in this context, both of them meaning that the project needs to meet defined *stakeholder** requirements.

Project work is rarely ever done within a single part of an organisation, e.g. contained within one department or using a single specialist group. Project work cuts across traditional boundaries and requires people to come together temporarily to focus on achieving the specific project objectives. As a result effective teamwork is central to projects.

Doing new things means that the outcomes can never be predicted with certainty. Uncertain situations are all around us, but the nature of project work means that there tends to be lots of uncertainty that might affect the project. For example, it is not possible to know with any degree of certainty how long it will take to create a new design or to build something that uses new technology.

---

* Stakeholders – the organisations or people who have an interest or role in the project or are impacted by the project.

Likewise it is not possible to know if a team who have not worked together before will be effective, or whether a new product, e.g. a Formula One racing car, will perform until it is actually tested.

All of the points made so far help define project work as distinct from other sorts of work. Most organisations will be able to separate those tasks that are done to maintain business-as-usual or operational activities from those things that are done to introduce change, i.e. projects.

The final way in which projects are different from the routine business of work is associated with the uniqueness of projects. While routine work involves the repetition of processes in a way that gives consistency and reliability, project work involves doing new things, or modifying existing methods and practices. This means that project work, unlike business-as-usual, will always have a defined start and an end point and a particular and unique piece of work to do between those points.

Taking all these considerations together, a project can be said to have the following features:

- it is a unique endeavour with defined start and finish points
- it is undertaken to achieve specific objectives for change
- it is carried out within defined time, cost and quality constraints
- it requires team-working across traditional departmental boundaries
- it necessarily involves uncertainty that needs to be managed.

Business-as-usual does not meet these criteria.

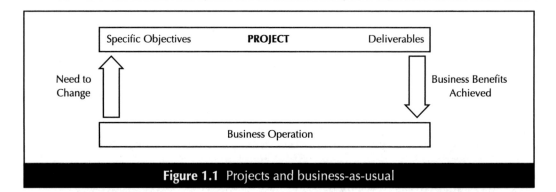

Figure 1.1 Projects and business-as-usual

Project Red Nose Day

You have been approached by a friend to be part of this year's national fund-raising programme for Comic Relief on Red Nose Day. You work in the headquarters building of a company along with 500 other people. Your friend would like you to organise fund-raising events to take place during normal working hours in exactly ten weeks' time. This coincides with national TV coverage of Red Nose Day. Your initial objectives from the national charity are to involve as many people as possible and to raise at least £10,000 for the charity.

Personal reflection

Think about organisations you know well, whether they are formally managed or informal ones such as your local football club or salsa class.

Think about how 'business-as-usual' works for each organisation and then contrast this with how change is managed by looking at how each of the points below applies to a project but does not apply to routine operations:

- a unique endeavour with defined start and finish points
- undertaken to achieve specific objectives for change
- carried out within defined time, cost and quality constraints
- requiring team-working across traditional departmental boundaries
- necessarily involving uncertainty that needs to be managed.

Write a short description of one project you know, illustrating the points in the bulleted list.

_____

_____

_____

_____

_____

_____

_____

_____

_____

DEFINE PROJECT MANAGEMENT

If projects are used to introduce change, then it follows logically that **project management** is primarily about controlling the introduction of the desired change.

The words or phrases that tend to be used to describe project management include:

- understanding the needs of all the stakeholders
- planning what work needs to be done, when, by whom and to what standards
- building and motivating the team to achieve the planned work
- coordinating the work of a range of different people
- monitoring that the work is being done to plan

- taking action to keep the planned work on track, or to change the plan in a controlled way if that is the best way to achieve the change objectives
- delivering successful results!

Project management should be a service to the organisation that is requesting the change, and is the process by which control is exerted over the project in order to achieve a desired end point.

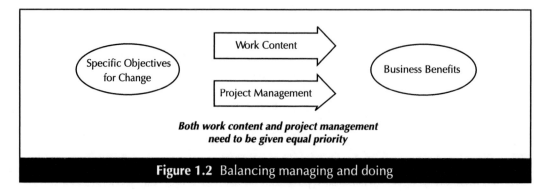

Figure 1.2 Balancing managing and doing

Some projects have a dedicated project manager who takes responsibility for delivering the project objectives to time, cost and quality. Where this is the case it will be easy to see that the work the project manager does is focused on the points in the bulleted list above.

Some projects have a project manager who additionally takes on the role of a technical specialist within the project team, e.g. a business analyst who is both managing the project to establish feasibility for a new computer system, and doing the business analysis themselves, or a manager of a hockey team who is both managing the organisation of a major tournament and playing in the tournament on the day.

When this happens – and it does all the time when projects are small or contained primarily within one part of the organisation – it is really important that the project manager focuses just as much on the management of the project as on completing the work that must be done for the project to be a success.

Project Red Nose Day

You are the project manager for Project Red Nose Day (RND). It is your responsibility to plan what needs to be done, making use of as many of the staff members as is practical. As you are an expert in communications management you will probably design and carry out the communications element of the project yourself. It is clearly your responsibility to monitor the work as it progresses, as well as motivate and coordinate your project team.

Personal reflection

Think about the work that project managers around you carry out and in particular think about project managers who are not 'full-time' on their projects, i.e. they are also one of the resources needed to complete the project activities.

Think about how they divide their time between 'managing' and 'doing work' for the project.

Reflect on each of the points below to see what needs to be managed if projects are to achieve their objectives:

- planning what work needs to be done, when, by whom and to what standards
- motivating the team to achieve the planned work
- coordinating the work of a range of different people
- monitoring that the work is being done to plan
- taking action to keep the planned work on track, or to change the plan in a controlled way if that is the best way to achieve the organisation's change objectives.

Write a short description of the management of a project you know, illustrating the points in the bulleted list.

_____

_____

_____

_____

_____

_____

_____

_____

_____

_____

DEFINE PROJECT MANAGEMENT PROCESSES

Processes are things that turn inputs into outputs.

It follows, then, that *project management processes* turn inputs, including things such as user requirements or technical specifications, into those outputs that will achieve the specific change objectives, e.g. new products or services.

Project management processes include:

- a starting or initiating process that secures agreement to begin a portion of work
- a planning process that initially takes an input such as an approved *business case** and turns it into a set of integrated plans against which to implement

* Business case – provides justification for undertaking a project. Its purpose is to obtain management commitment and approval for investment in the project.

the project; as the project progresses there is invariably a need for a replanning process to reflect project progress or changes in objectives

- a monitoring process that measures the progress of a project against its plan, whether it is ahead or behind schedule, overspending or underspending against budget or delivering outputs that meet the desired performance or quality objectives
- a controlling process that reacts to the information gathered during monitoring and enables decisions to be made to correct lateness, overspending or poor quality
- a learning process that takes an input such as a finished project and turns it into a set of amended guidelines, processes and checklists for the next project
- a closing process that formally concludes a portion of work and hands it over to business-as-usual.

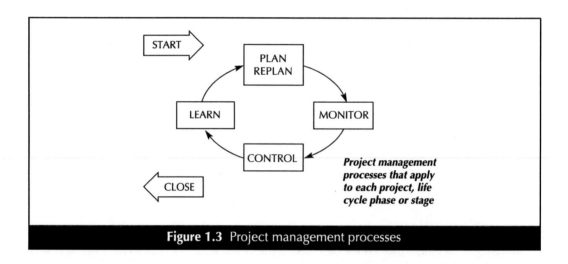

Figure 1.3 Project management processes

You will see a pattern among these processes which is that they are not specific to any particular project or any project *phase**: rather, they are the things that happen on all projects and in all phases of a project. They are the things concerned with project management, rather than 'doing' the work.

The labels and terms used to describe a particular process may vary. Sometimes it is easy to become confused between the labels given for project management processes and the labels given for project phases. This will be explored further in Chapter 4, which deals with the project life cycle.

The fact is that theoretical terms rarely matter. What does matter in practice is not only that you understand the terms that are used in your organisation, but also that you can compare and contrast them with other terms used in published literature about project management as a means of understanding what your organisation does and why.

---

* Phase – the part of a project during which a set of related and interlinked activities are performed to attain a designated objective.

> **Project Red Nose Day**
>
> Your project to raise money for the Comic Relief charity is made up of six distinct phases: pre-authorisation, consultation with staff, designing the events to take place, communication, the 'day' itself and collecting donations. These phases make up the project life cycle for your project.
>
> To apply project management processes, each phase needs to be started, planned, monitored, controlled and closed, with any lessons learned for future projects.

Personal reflection

Think about the projects that you are familiar with in your workplace or in your social or family life.

Think about what project management processes are carried out and how. What names are given to these processes?

Ask yourself how each of the processes below needs to be controlled if a project is to achieve its objectives:

- starting or initiating
- planning
- monitoring
- controlling
- learning
- closing

Write a short description of the use of project management processes on a project you know, illustrating the points in the bulleted list.

_____

_____

_____

_____

_____

_____

_____

_____

DEFINE THE RELATIONSHIP BETWEEN TIME, COST AND QUALITY

Time, cost and quality are the three attributes that are typically described as either objectives or constraints for any project. For example:

- the project must be completed by 31 December 2008
- the project must not spend more than £500,000
- the products and services created must meet specification X456.

Sometimes these attributes are alternatively stated as schedule, budget and performance, but here we will refer to time, cost and quality. The relationship between these three attributes is at the heart of project management.

It is unlikely that any project could ever achieve objectives that are considered to be the quickest, the cheapest and the best. In fact, if a project has to be delivered to meet a challenging finish date, it is likely that it will cost more than if it had a more relaxed schedule. Likewise, if a project has to achieve a tight specification for quality, it will probably cost more or take longer than it would have if the quality requirements had been reduced. Taking this into account, it is no surprise that projects that involve public safety tend to take longer and cost more than originally planned. Similarly, projects that need to be completed by a certain date, perhaps building a new stadium for a planned sporting event, almost invariably cost more than planned and have a finished product that is to a lower specification than was originally conceived.

Projects are unique, and initial plans that reflect time, cost and quality objectives are, in reality, 'educated guesses' that need to be implemented in an uncertain world. In such a scenario it is rare for the project to proceed exactly to plan. The more usual situation is that something happens that requires the project manager to make a 'trade-off' – to take more time to achieve the specification, to spend more money to hold the deadline or to agree reduced quality in order to hold the time and cost plans.

Because such dilemmas typify project management, the triangular relationship between time, cost and quality is often called the 'iron triangle of project management' or the 'project manager's trilemma'.

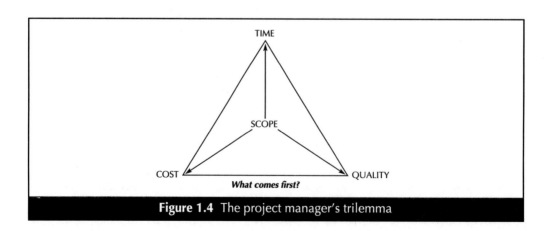

Figure 1.4 The project manager's trilemma

Often the area inside the triangle is said to represent the project *scope*, i.e. all the work that has to be done to achieve the time, cost and quality objectives. This is clearly another attribute of the project that can be varied as long as the project manager can be certain that an amended scope will still deliver the benefits that the organisation requires from the change. A reduction in scope means that less work will be done which then makes time and cost objectives more achievable.

It follows, then, that the most important thing for a project manager to understand when balancing the time, cost and quality objectives is the relative priority of objectives for the client organisation. Is it more important to finish on time, on budget or to the right quality?

Project Red Nose Day

National RND will take place in exactly ten weeks. This date is not moveable. You have talked to your boss, who is the HR director. She supports the project and has agreed to act as *sponsor** but has introduced the following new constraints within which you must manage the project:

- whatever you do must not offend anyone
- the whole project must not eat up more than 1000 hours of work time for staff, including you
- there should be no more than £500 of external expenditure
- the company should get good press through local newspaper, radio and TV coverage.

Given this information, you understand the relative priorities to be: time, because the date is fixed; cost, because your boss has given you an effective maximum budget; and then quality (in terms of positive awareness generated and funds raised), as no promises have been made to the national charity.

Personal reflection

Think about the projects that you are familiar with in your workplace or in your social or family life.

Think about how time, cost and quality objectives either potentially or actually conflict. Reflect on how important it is for the project manager to understand the relative priority of time, cost and quality in the context of the work to be done if project objectives are to be achieved.

Briefly describe how the 'trilemma' of the 'iron triangle' has practically affected projects that you are familiar with, and what actions were taken to make sure that the change objectives of the organisation were protected.

---

* Sponsor – the individual or body for whom the project is undertaken and who is the primary risk-taker. The sponsor owns the business case and is ultimately accountable for the project and for delivering the benefits.

_____

_____

_____

_____

_____

_____

_____

_____

Programme management 2 and portfolio management

Topics 1.2 and 1.3 in the *APM Body of Knowledge* deal with programmes and programme management and with portfolios and portfolio management. The words programme and portfolio have multiple meanings both in general and in business. It is therefore important to understand what these terms mean in relation to project management. Both programmes and portfolios are each distinct from projects, and many people working on projects in organisations will recognise that their project is part of a wider programme or portfolio. It follows then that understanding what programmes and portfolios are and what they are meant to achieve is important background for those starting out in project management.

DEFINE A PROGRAMME AND PROGRAMME MANAGEMENT

Programme is a collective term for either a group of projects or a group of projects and routine work with a common purpose. A few years ago, 'programme' was used to describe any collection of projects, but modern thinking has now moved on to clearly differentiate between projects, programmes and portfolios. Portfolios will be described in the next section.

A programme is not just a large project. In a large project, such as designing and building the Channel Tunnel or designing and building a power station, it is possible to identify the work to be done at the start, even if that work will take many years to complete. The work isn't optional: to achieve the stated specification all the work needs to be done.

In a programme, such as the merger of two companies or a major restructuring of a business, it is possible to focus on the end goal, but it is not possible at the outset to identify all the work that will need to be done to get there. Projects will be done in phases and when the business goal has been achieved, work will stop. Programmes are much more ambiguous than projects, and programme management involves some different skills from project management.

Programme management involves coordinating work across multiple projects and business-as-usual in order to bring about beneficial change, usually of a strategic nature, for an organisation.

This description suggests that programme management is about doing the right work to achieve the high-level benefits, rather than just focusing on the projects within the programme delivering their time, cost and quality objectives. As a result programme managers focus on facilitating and leading change, and leave the work of project management to the project managers. Often the

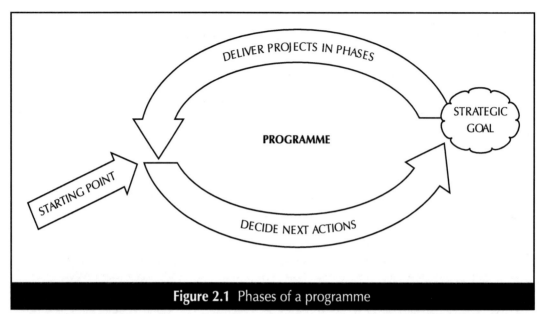

Figure 2.1 Phases of a programme

programme manager will take the role of the sponsor for the projects within the programme.

Programme management is needed to make sure that the right projects and other work are chosen so that the organisation achieves the strategic benefits. It provides clear linkage between projects and business goals so work is not wasteful and attention is not diverted to work that is not essential. It also manages the interfaces between projects and maintains a clear focus on the future benefits. The projects within the programme concentrate on delivering their specific objectives.

Project Red Nose Day

The local RND project that you are managing is part of the Comic Relief charity's annual fund-raising campaign, or annual programme. The aim of this year's campaign, like all others, is to raise a significant amount of money for the causes that it supports. Local RND projects like yours form a key part of this programme along with other projects such as a pop single and calendar, as well as the ongoing work of selling Red Nose memorabilia. The RND programme manager is always looking for other good ideas to assist in achieving the strategic objective of raising lots of money. It is likely that a number of new projects will be added to the programme and, depending on their contribution to the financial target, these may well replace existing projects that have already been started.

Personal reflection

Think of an example from your personal experience that could be described as a programme rather than a project.

What were the features of this example that made it a programme and not just a large project?

Can you think of ways in which the work and role of a programme manager differs from the work and role of a project manager?

_____

_____

_____

_____

_____

_____

_____

_____

_____

DEFINE A PORTFOLIO AND PORTFOLIO MANAGEMENT

A **portfolio** is a grouping or bundle of projects and/or programmes collected together for management convenience under the sponsorship of an organisation, or a specific part of an organisation.

Portfolios of projects are often related only by the use of common resources. An example of a portfolio of projects would be all the work taking place in a company's IT department during the next financial year. Although some of the projects may share the same strategic objective, many of them are unrelated except that they share a common resource pool and are taking place within the same time frame. Another example would be all the projects being undertaken by a railway maintenance contractor working in one regional area. Many of the projects that make up this portfolio will be geographically separated but will still use the same resources.

Portfolios of programmes are related because they represent the collection of work being carried by a whole organisation or significant subset of an organisation. An example of a portfolio of programmes would be all the change-related work taking place within a government department such as the Department for Education and Skills.

Where programmes are said to have a common goal, portfolios of projects and portfolios of programmes can both be said to have a common theme.

Portfolio management is the selection and management of groups of projects and other work at either functional (departmental) or organisational levels taking into account resource constraints. Because a portfolio has a common theme and not a common goal, as in the case of a programme, the priorities for management are different.

The most important concept here is that the management of a portfolio gives an organisation a method to manage resource constraints by making sure that precious and scarce resources are used in the most efficient way possible. This

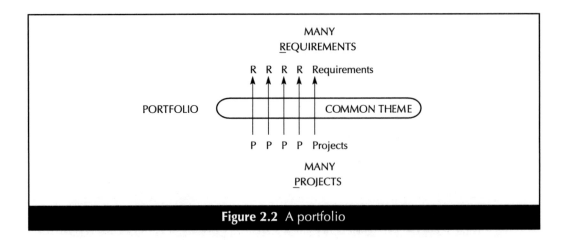

Figure 2.2 A portfolio

can be done only if priorities can be defined between projects (or programmes) in a portfolio. Setting priorities and making tough decisions about how resources will be used is therefore the most essential aspect of portfolio management.

Project Red Nose Day

Although you have accepted the role of project manager for the RND project you also have a number of other projects and routine jobs to do. Within the next three months you need to prepare a detailed presentation on how the company can improve its project management processes for presentation to the business change steering committee. You also want to find somewhere else to live as you are unhappy in your rented flat, and you want to research and book a holiday.

If RND, project management improvements, moving to a new place and your holiday are considered as four projects, then what you are managing overall is a portfolio. The projects in this portfolio are linked together by two aspects: firstly they are taking place in the same time frame, and secondly they share a common resource – YOU. They do not have a common goal but they have a common theme. Thinking of the four projects as a group (portfolio), along with your usual work, will help you to plan and manage your time most efficiently.

Personal reflection

Think of an example of a portfolio from your own experience, or from observing others at work.

What were the features of this example that made it a portfolio, rather than a programme or a large project?

Can you think of ways in which the work of a portfolio manager differs from the work of a project manager, or of a programme manager?

3 Organisational roles

Topic 6.8 in the *APM Body of Knowledge* deals with the role and responsibilities of a number of key positions within any project. Each of these roles has specific meaning within a project context and so it is important to understand each one of them and to be able to differentiate the associated responsibilities. It will also help to realise that no one person involved in a project is responsible for everything. In addition to organisational roles, topic 1.5 of the *Body of Knowledge* deals specifically with the role of project sponsorship. The fact that the *Body of Knowledge* treats this topic separately emphasises its importance in making a project successful, but for present purposes it is included in this chapter.

DEFINE THE DIFFERENT ROLES AND RESPONSIBILITIES REQUIRED IN THE MANAGEMENT OF PROJECTS

There are five primary roles that are required in order to effectively manage a project.

- The **project manager**: the individual with the authority, accountability and day-to-day responsibility for delivering the project in line with its specific objectives, including time, cost and quality. The project manager owns the *project management plan (PMP)** and is accountable to the sponsor for effective implementation of that plan.
- The **sponsor** (sometimes called project executive): the individual for whom the project is undertaken, the primary risk-taker. The sponsor owns the business case and is ultimately accountable to the senior management of the organisation who is doing the work for delivering the benefits from the project. The term **sponsorship** is used to describe what a sponsor does. The responsibility of the sponsor is to ensure that the project remains a viable proposition and that benefits are realised, resolving any *issues** outside the control of the project manager.

---

* Project management plan (PMP) – a document that brings together all the plans for a project. The purpose of the PMP is to document the outcome of the planning process and to provide the reference document for managing the project.

* Issue – a current concern or threat to the project objectives that cannot be resolved by the project manager.

- The **user** or senior user: the person who represents the group of people who are intended to use the project outputs for the benefit of the organisation. One responsibility of the user is to define requirements and *acceptance criteria**.
- The **project team member**: someone who is allocated work to perform on the project and who is responsible to the project manager for that work, irrespective of who their 'normal' line manager might be. Project team members can be staff of the organisation, suppliers, contractors, consultants or in some rarer cases members of the customer's organisation. Project team members may be more junior or more senior to the project manager, but for that project they must take direction from him or her.
- The **steering group** (sometimes called project board): the people representing the senior management of the organisation investing in the project. The senior user will be a member of the project steering group along with senior functional (departmental) managers who provide resources for the project and also other representatives of key stakeholders. The senior functional managers are sometimes called senior suppliers. The sponsor is chosen by and is accountable to the project steering group and also typically chairs the meetings of the group. The project steering group must provide strategic direction and guidance to the sponsor, and in doing so provide clarity of purpose for the project manager and their project team members.

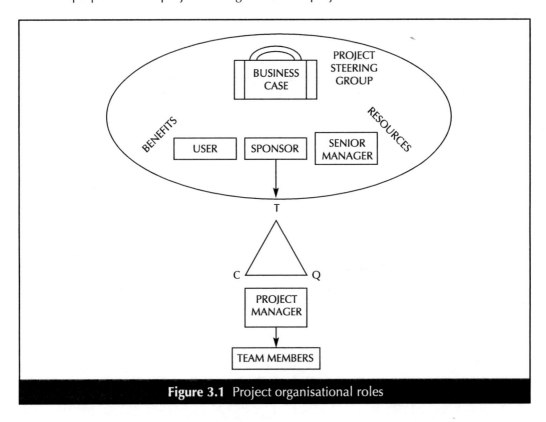

Figure 3.1 Project organisational roles

* Acceptance criteria – the requirements and essential conditions that have to be achieved before project deliverables are accepted.

The first three of these roles – project manager, sponsor and user – are essential to all projects. Sometimes a project manager may be asked to take on the responsibilities of the sponsor and/or user as well as their own; this is not effective. Only if each role is fulfilled by different people can the internal contradictions and conflicting requirements of the project be effectively managed.

Project Red Nose Day

The key roles for the project have been identified. You are the project manager and your boss is the sponsor. You and the sponsor have decided that the user should ideally be a staff representative who is not part of the organising group. Team members include the health and safety officer, the security adviser, the event managers, the finance manager and the quality manager. You will hold a meeting of all these people to discuss the PMP and to ask them to agree and sign off the content.

You haven't decided if you need a steering group, but if you do it will include your boss as sponsor, a user (staff representative) and probably the managing director, as he is a key stakeholder and will want to be involved.

Personal reflection

Think about projects you know well.

Reflect on how the roles of the sponsor, project manager and user are different, even if they are performed by the same person.

Briefly describe your views on where roles could be combined, and where they should be kept separate, and explain why.

Project life cycles 4

Topic 6.1 in the *APM Body of Knowledge* deals with the definition and phases of a project life cycle and explains the reasons for splitting projects into phases. The idea of a life cycle is one of the things that makes project work different from business-as-usual. You could say that all projects have a start, middle and end, whereas business-as-usual has only a middle. As is often the case in project management the labels used to describe the phases of a life cycle are never as simple as start, middle and end. There are many different labels given to the phases within a life cycle depending on where you work and the history of the organisation. The key thing is to understand the purpose of the life cycle phases and not to worry about the different terminology used. You only need to understand the terms used in the organisation(s) you work within.

DEFINE A PROJECT LIFE CYCLE AND PROJECT LIFE CYCLE PHASES

Using a **life cycle** allows a project to be considered as a sequence of **phases** which provides the structure and approach for delivering one distinct chunk of work at a time and ensuring that nothing has been missed.

Many life cycles are depicted as steps going down or as a waterfall. Sometimes life cycles are depicted as a straight line, a 'V' or a spiral, but these are less often used.

A commonly used project life cycle might include these four phases in this sequence:

Concept
>Definition
>>Implementation
>>>Handover and closeout

However, it is usual for organisations to use different terms for life cycle phases, e.g. concept is sometimes called initiation, definition sometimes called planning and implementation sometimes called execution. Often, as in the case in our Red Nose Day case study, life cycle phases relate specifically to the project.

You will see from these words, though, that the labelling of life cycle phases is a potentially confusing area when starting out in project management. The main thing to understand is the reason for splitting projects into life cycle phases as a way of controlling the project as effectively as possible. The benefits of using a life cycle are outlined in the next section.

Project Red Nose Day

You have decided that your project to raise money for the Comic Relief charity is made up of six distinct phases: pre-authorisation, consultation with staff, designing the events to take place, communication, preparation for and the 'day' itself and collecting donations. Figure 4.1 illustrates the life cycle of the RND project.

Mapping the RND project life cycle to the commonly used life cycle above you could say that the pre-authorisation and consultation with staff phases are part of 'concept'. Designing the events is part of 'definition'. Communication and the day itself are part of 'implementation', and collecting donations is part of 'handover and closeout'.

Personal reflection

Think about projects that you have worked on, either at work or socially.

What were the project life cycle phases that were defined? Did they vary from project to project or remain constant?

Briefly describe the benefits of using a life cycle from your own perspective.

_____

_____

_____

_____

_____

_____

_____

_____

_____

_____

DEFINE THE REASONS FOR SPLITTING PROJECTS INTO PHASES

All projects should be managed using a life cycle for the following reasons:

- the life cycle divides the project into manageable pieces or phases
- it provides a mechanism to continually review what has actually happened, compared to the plan, and to make sure that the business case is still valid
- it ensures that the early phases of a project are not ignored
- treating each phase of the project as a mini-project will ensure that each phase is itself started correctly, planned, monitored and closed with lessons learned for the future

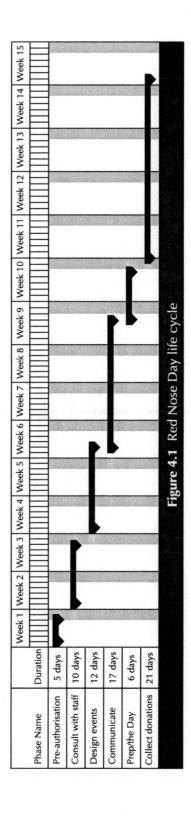

Figure 4.1 Red Nose Day life cycle

- the life cycle assists in project planning and, in particular, in scheduling and estimating
- resources can be allocated to each phase and, as a result, resource shortages or clashes across projects can be predicted
- the life cycle provides a means of reporting project status using a consistent set of terms and phase descriptions
- it encourages interim project reviews at the end of each phase
- it facilitates formal 'go/no-go' decision-making at the end of each phase.

The last bullet point is particularly important. It means that a project will never be able to pass from being just 'a good idea' to a completed product without a number of checks and balances. Typical phase review points or project gates might take place after

- production of the initial business case
- production of the project management plan (PMP)
- completion of design
- completion of a pilot

or before:

- awarding major contracts
- starting major building works
- starting a major roll-out.

At each go/no-go decision point the current project status or health should be compared to the current approved business case. This will itself help in the review and approval process. It is the sponsor's role to ensure that the appropriate level of approval is gained to proceed to the next project phase, assuming that they cannot give approval themselves.

Effective implementation of the go/no-go decision points will ensure that only those projects that should go ahead actually do so and those that should be cancelled are actually stopped. This means in turn that more projects will be successful in delivering the benefits they set out to achieve.

Project Red Nose Day

Considering the life cycle as shown in Figure 4.2, phase review points or project gate reviews should take place after

- staff consultation is complete and the business case is agreed
- the event design and project management plan are agreed
- the RND day is complete
- donations are collected.

Personal reflection

Further consider the life cycles used on projects you are familiar with.

Was the life cycle used to facilitate decision-making at defined points or gateways?

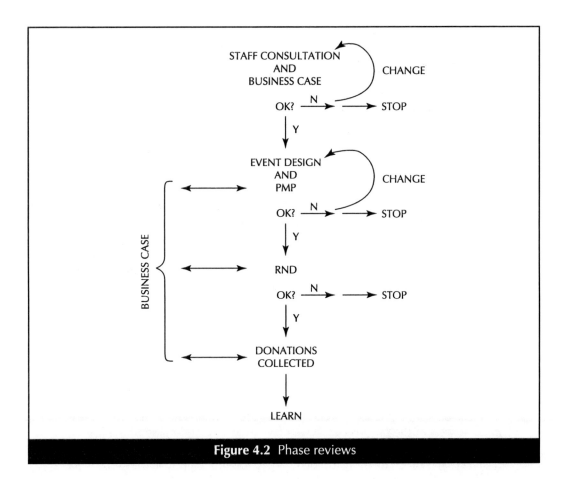

Figure 4.2 Phase reviews

Briefly describe your views on the need for phase review and approval, and the methods used to achieve them in your experience.

5 Project context

Topic 1.4 in the *APM Body of Knowledge* deals with the subject of project context and the importance of understanding the various aspects that influence the project. You could say that the project context is the world in which the project is being carried out. As we live in an ever-changing world we must be continually aware of what is going on around us. As Figure 5.1 illustrates below – either understand the project context, or work in the dark!

DEFINE PROJECT CONTEXT

The key point here is that understanding the ***project context*** (sometimes called project environment) helps with planning the project. This is because numerous factors from a project's wider context or environment can have an influence. Understanding these factors and how they influence a project will assist in all aspects of the project's management, such as planning, communication and delivery. It is important to understand two dimensions of context: first, the context that is internal to the company or organisation carrying out the project, e.g. the political sensitivity of the project; second, the context that is external to the project or organisation, i.e. the environment into which the project will be delivered.

There are a number of tools and techniques that can be used to understand the internal and external environment or project context. What they all have in common is a focus on the things that matter to stakeholders.

Different stakeholders care about different issues – financial or economic, technical or technology based, social or political. Others may care about the legality or environmental 'friendliness' of the project. If the project manager does not understand the project context then they are attempting to achieve project objectives in a vacuum.

If a project manager fails to consider the context, the uncertainty leaves the project exposed to an increased level of *risk**. The risks may be managed successfully, but in practice it is safe to say that projects that are not grounded in a good understanding of the wider context tend to fail. Ignoring reality doesn't work.

---

* Risk (event) – an uncertain future event or set of circumstances whose occurrence would have an effect on the achievement of one or more of the project objectives.

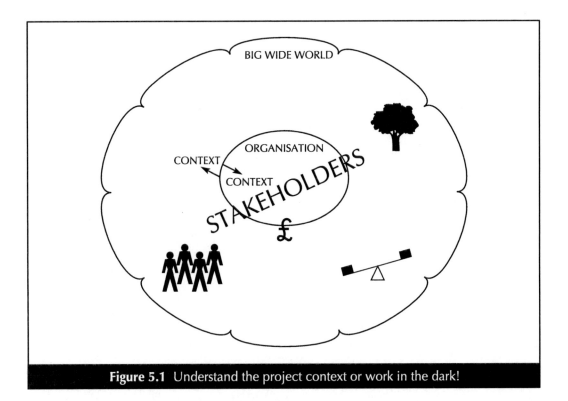

Figure 5.1 Understand the project context or work in the dark!

The acronym PESTLE can be used as a way of analysing and understanding the context of a project, and it provides a usable and effective structure for thinking about the wider environment into which the project must deliver. The acronym stands for the following factors:

- political
- economic
- sociological
- technical
- legal
- environmental (green).

Consider this example of building a new tram system in a major city. *Politically*, the project may be seen as a 'pet project' for the current local authority as it is part of an initiative to improve inner city redevelopment. *Economically*, the project might be dependent on favourable private financing and will be linked to interest rates. *Socially*, the project will be seen as a means of removing cars from the city centre and hence improving public access and reducing journey times. If the project is being undertaken in a city centre that has narrow streets or is quite hilly, then from a *technical* perspective there might be some problems. The compulsory purchase of land or the disruption to business may mean that the project is *legally* challenged. And, finally, such a project is almost certain to have an *environmental* aspect to the context as it will reduce pollution and noise levels during operation.

Project Red Nose Day

Understanding the context in which you must deliver the RND project will help you in its management. Although Comic Relief is a national charity that most people in the company are aware of and will support, there are likely to be a few who actively support other charities and will not appreciate being asked to support this one. You will need to be politically sensitive when addressing this. The amount of money that you raise will be affected by the economic situation at the time. If the event day falls just after everyone has been paid, you might end up raising quite a lot more than expected. You also want to ensure that the individual events you plan are socially acceptable and don't cause any embarrassment or injury. You don't see any technical issues with the project, but you are concerned with possible legal obligations and therefore you will be talking to the company lawyer in advance. You will certainly make sure that you have good insurance cover. None of the events that you are currently contemplating will have any major environmental aspects. You will make sure that any rubbish or waste is properly disposed of and you will think about this further as you proceed to put together your plans.

Personal reflection

Think about a project that you are familiar with. What aspects of the project context or environment were considered at the start of the project?

Were there aspects of the context that were not considered that caused problems later on with the project?

Write a short description of the context of a project you are familiar with, using the six PESTLE headings for guidance.

_____

_____

_____

_____

_____

_____

_____

_____

_____

_____

Stakeholder management 6

Topic 2.2 in the *APM Body of Knowledge* deals with stakeholders, stakeholder management and stakeholder analysis. It is widely accepted that understanding and engaging with stakeholders is really important for successful project management and should not be overlooked. A project manager needs to make sure that all stakeholders are identified and, where required, actively managed. Key stakeholders don't tend to go away, so ignoring them usually causes problems of some description for the project.

DEFINE STAKEHOLDER AND STAKEHOLDER MANAGEMENT

A ***stakeholder*** is a person or group of people who have a role to play in, are interested in or are affected by the project in some way. In terms of project management a stakeholder is often described as anyone or any organisation that can help or hinder the project.

Understanding who stakeholders are and their needs is a very important aspect of project management and one of the key duties of the project manager. If stakeholder needs and expectations are understood from the start, the project manager can then communicate with these people in an appropriate way as the project progresses. Keeping stakeholders 'on side' and supportive of the project is an essential skill. This skill is what is formally called ***stakeholder management***.

Some stakeholders may not be very interested in the project at the start, but are very influential – for example, the union or staff representative. Their influence may begin to affect the project if one of their members should become aggrieved. Other stakeholders may be very interested in the project, but not very influential. For example, a manager in a department that is not involved in the project might want to see how the change will be implemented so they can consider something similar in future. These stakeholders need to be managed in addition to those who are both interested and influential from the start. Things change, and when they do the project manager needs to know who can help and who might hinder.

If understanding stakeholders is critical to effective project management, then it follows that stakeholder management should be a systematic part of the project manager's job. Engaging with stakeholders throughout the project life cycle is a key action to ensure that project communication works.

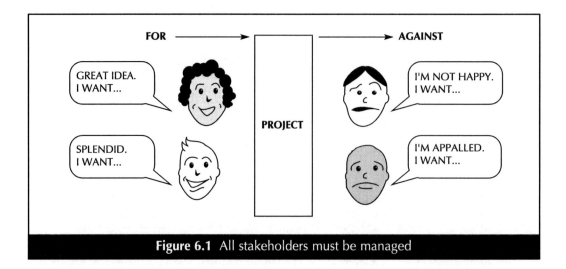

Figure 6.1 All stakeholders must be managed

Project Red Nose Day

There are a number of obvious stakeholders in this project. All those employed in the head office are stakeholders because you want to involve them all in the activities on the day. Some of them are stakeholders in other ways. For example, your boss is a key stakeholder as she has set out some constraints for the project which she will want you to adhere to, and she is the sponsor. The company's managing director is also a stakeholder as he will not want anything to go wrong that might affect company performance. Company employees who have agreed to take part in organising and running the events you plan, and therefore might be a little concerned as to what they are letting themselves in for, are also stakeholders. You are a key stakeholder too. Other stakeholders will include those involved in the national Red Nose Day programme, although their interest is actually likely to be quite low.

Knowing who the stakeholders are will enable you to manage them, e.g. if you want to put your participants' minds at ease you should let them know what you are thinking of doing and get their input as early as possible.

Personal reflection

Think about a project you know well and the stakeholders for the project.

What methods were used to identify stakeholders and find out their needs and expectations?

Write a short description of stakeholders in a project you know, showing how they were managed so that they helped, rather than hindered, the project.

_____

_____

_____

_____

_____

_____

_____

_____

_____

DEFINE STAKEHOLDER ANALYSIS

Because stakeholder identification and management is important, project managers and their team need to have ways of understanding what stakeholders think about the project. Most people do this using some form of stakeholder analysis.

One simple way of doing **stakeholder analysis** is, for each identified stakeholder, to consider three things. First, what their interest is in the project; second, whether or not they can influence the project; and third, whether their attitude to the project is for or against. It is clear that those stakeholders who are very interested in the delivery of the forecasted benefits and are influential enough to make the change happen are very important. This is irrespective of whether their attitude is positive or negative. Their views need to be considered and any risks they identify, or issues they are aware of, should be explicitly addressed in the project management plan (PMP).

An example of such a group of interested and influential stakeholders might be the department affected by the introduction of new working practices. The introduction of the new practices may unavoidably lead to some job losses. It will also mean new ways of working, using new systems and processes. It is those remaining in the department who will have to use the new systems and processes. If they are consulted during the preparation of the business case they may identify risks such as 'key retained staff may not like the new ways of working and will leave of their own accord'. They may also identify issues such as 'staff are very concerned about the lack of information available and are also worried about job security'. The risks and issues identified should be considered when assessing the business case and when it is taken forward into the definition phase of the project.

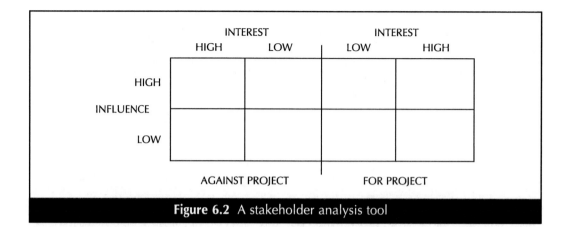

Figure 6.2 A stakeholder analysis tool

Project Red Nose Day

There are a number of key stakeholders in the project, including you, the sponsor, team members and event participants. No real stakeholder analysis has been carried out so far, so you know you need to do this and you think a good time would be as part of the staff consultation phase of the project life cycle. If any significant points arise then they can be fed into the business case and PMP. It would have been good to do this work earlier, but it is better to think about stakeholders late than not at all.

Personal reflection

Further consider the projects you are familiar with at work.

How were stakeholder views taken into consideration when putting together the business case and plans?

Briefly describe your views on the importance of stakeholder analysis as a tool for influencing the management of the project. What are the main problems to be overcome in practice?

Project success and 7
benefits management

Topic 2.1 in the *APM Body of Knowledge* deals with defining and measuring project success, with success factors for projects and with the subject of benefits management. This is another area of project management where the terms can be confusing because different organisations often use different labels for the same things. Knowing what success looks like, and knowing you have achieved it, is fundamental to project management, so all the terms need to be fully understood by all those involved in projects.

DEFINE PROJECT SUCCESS CRITERIA, KEY PERFORMANCE INDICATORS (KPIS) AND BENEFITS

Project success criteria are the criteria by which the success of a project will be judged. Without success criteria, any project that is actually completed could be argued to be a success, irrespective of whether it was delivered on time, to budget or to the agreed quality criteria.

The project's time, cost and quality objectives will inevitably form at least some of the project's success criteria. For example, for the project to be successful, it should:

- be complete by 31 December 2008
- cost no more than £500,000
- deliver products and services that meet specification X456.

Some projects warrant additional success criteria, e.g. all employees who remain with the company after the reorganisation are happy in their new jobs, or everybody who takes the examination passes.

While some people will differentiate between *objective*, i.e. a predetermined result towards which effort is directed, and *success criteria*, i.e. the criteria against which success of the project may be judged, for the purposes of this book the terms are used interchangeably.

If success criteria are those aspects of the project that matter to stakeholders and will be used to judge whether the project was successful or not, then it makes sense that they need to be measured and monitored as the project progresses through the life cycle.

Key performance indicators (KPIs) can be defined as the measures that are indicative of whether the project is progressing towards a successful conclusion or not. KPIs are used to establish a measurement baseline at the start of project so that progress can be monitored throughout and success judged at the end of the project. This is easy for tangible things, such as 'cost no more than £500,000', but it is more difficult for less tangible success criteria, such as 'employees are happy in their new jobs'.

It would be convenient for the project to concentrate on things that are easy to measure and ignore the others, but this would be a mistake. Creative ways of measuring those less tangible criteria that inevitably reflect the success of the project need to be found.

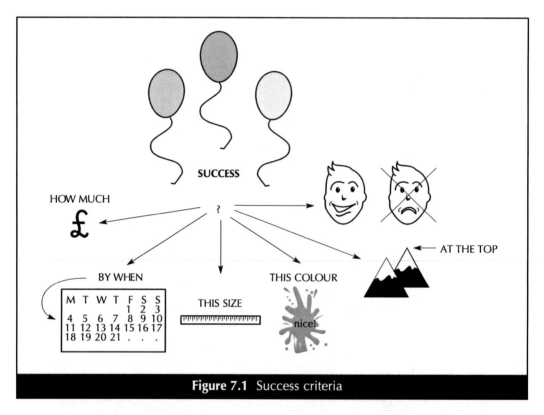

Figure 7.1 Success criteria

Use of the term 'benefit' alongside success criteria within project management is becoming more popular.

Benefits are typically defined as quantifiable improvements, of value to stakeholders, resulting from the completion of the project's *deliverables**.

At first glance this definition may seem very similar to our definition of project success criteria, but there is a difference. Project success criteria focus on the project, the things that the project manager has to deliver for the project to be successful. Benefits focus on the business, the things that the sponsor must achieve to be successful by taking the completed project deliverables, such as a new IT system, and realising benefit for the business through the use of that new system. These might include increased sales, better customer service or reduced costs, for example.

---

* Deliverables – the end products of a project or the measurable results of intermediate activities within the project organisation.

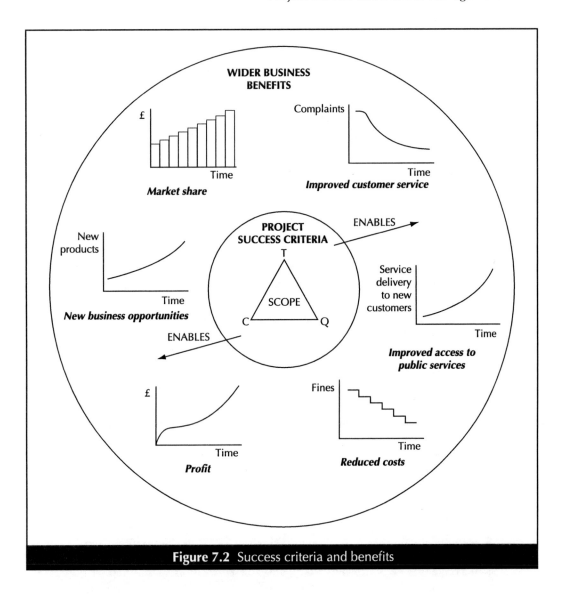

Figure 7.2 Success criteria and benefits

Project Red Nose Day

You have agreed that the success criteria for the RND project are as follows:

- the project is a workplace event and should involve as many people as possible
- it must take place in exactly ten weeks' time, and all the money donated should be received or collected within four weeks of the close of the event
- it must utilise no more than 1000 hours of company time, and require no more than an additional £500 of company expenditure

- it should aim to raise £10,000 for a range of charitable causes approved and supported by participating staff and the charity coordinating the national link-up to this event, Comic Relief
- there should be no complaints from staff about the events
- there should be no complaints from customers about reduced service as a result of staff participation in the events
- the company should get good press through local newspaper, radio and TV coverage
- when questioned after RND, 90% of staff will support an RND project next year.

It will be important to monitor progress towards the success criteria. Key performance indicators will include:

- the number of people actively taking part in the project on a day-to-day basis, including the number of volunteers to participate on the day itself
- the amount of time being expended on the project, as tracked by the company's time recording system
- the amount of money pledged to Comic Relief, as reported on a weekly basis
- the number of (or lack of) phone calls/emails received by HR from staff complaining about the event, as logged in the staff complaints book
- interest from local media, as measured by number of phone calls received.

The benefits of the RND project are:

- raising money for a well-respected and worthwhile charity
- increased staff morale, as measured by the annual staff survey showing that staff are happy in their work
- a higher ranking in the annual 'best place to work' report, which will encourage good people to want to join the company
- an increased public awareness of the company and positive impact on the company's image leading, hopefully but not measurably within this project, to increased sales.

Personal reflection

Think about a project you know well.
  What success criteria did the stakeholders ask for in addition to the time, cost and quality?
  How were the less tangible criteria described and measured?
  What KPIs were agreed?
  What other success criteria might there have been for this project?
  What benefits did this project provide for the organisation?

_____

_____

_____

_____

_____

_____

_____

_____

_____

DEFINE SUCCESS FACTORS

For projects to achieve their success criteria and deliver their desired benefits, it helps if a number of generic factors are in place. It is easy to spot when these factors are missing as there tends to be a feeling that the project is not going well, but when they are in place things feel good. These 'feel good' factors, when present in the project environment, positively help the achievement of a successful project: they are formally called **success factors**. If success factors are absent then the project is more likely to fail. Some would say that there are a number of success factors that are more important than others. These are often called critical success factors (CSFs) because if any one of them is absent the project will fail in one way or another.

Numerous lists of critical success factors have been produced by people writing in project management. Common to most lists are the following:

- *clear goals and objectives*, without which there will not be any clear understanding of what the project is setting out to achieve and what its objectives are
- *good sponsorship or senior management support* for the project, without which the project will find itself struggling to get committed resources and organisational buy-in
- *realistic plans* that can be followed and then used to monitor and control against
- *open consultation and communication* with all those involved, i.e. all stakeholders
- *a motivated and competent project team* that will both want to carry out the project and be able to deliver it.

It is difficult to actually measure whether or not critical success factors are in place but as mentioned above it is easy to spot when they are not. If any of the following occur then it is likely that one or more critical success factors are missing:

Figure 7.3 Critical success factors

- numerous requests for changes to the project scope, timescale, budget or quality objectives
- push-back from the users or those affected by the project
- missing of milestones, overspending or poor quality of deliverables
- arguments between the project manager and key stakeholders
- reducing numbers or poor behaviour at team meetings.

Project Red Nose Day

All of the success factors outlined above apply equally to the RND project. It is clear that if senior management remove their support then it is quite likely that those needed to participate will find other things to do. Likewise, if you as project manager find that key stakeholders are unclear about what you are doing then you have failed to have open communication with them.

Personal reflection

Think about a project you know well.

Can you see any evidence that any of the critical success factors are not in place?

If you can, what is happening as a result of their absence?

8 Communication

Topic 7.1 in the *APM Body of Knowledge* deals with communication on projects, the methods and media used to communicate with all those involved, and the importance and contents of the communication plan. Experienced project managers spend the vast majority of their time communicating in one form or another. Assuming this is true, then it follows that this is another foundational topic to consider when starting out in project management.

DEFINE COMMUNICATION AND THE CONTENTS OF THE COMMUNICATION PLAN

Communication is the transmission and receipt of information so that all parties receive and understand what the sender intends. Communication should never be a linear and one-way phenomenon. Others may interpret our words and actions differently from what was intended. It is also easy to assume similarity or even difference when none exists. Effective communication is rarely about the simple confirmation of a message.

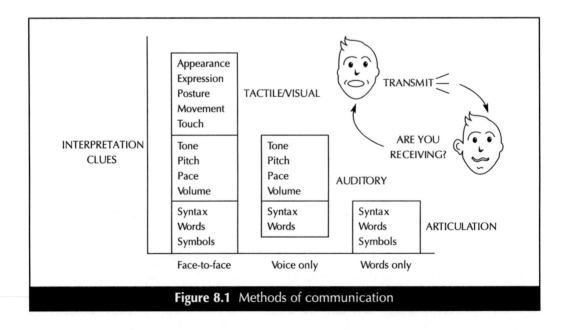

Figure 8.1 Methods of communication

Figure 8.1 explains three general categories for methods of communication and suggests how 'rich' the communication is using each method. For example, a face-to-face encounter with someone means that the whole range of verbal and non-verbal clues are available to be interpreted, whereas a telephone call restricts the clues to those that can be heard, and a letter or report to those clues that can be read. Choice of communication method and the medium used is really important if you are to be sure that the recipient understands the message you are intending to send.

Email as a communication method is increasingly used in organisations. Everyone will have their own examples of where their intention in sending an email was misunderstood by the receiver. In particular, people now use email to be more than a 'words only' method, attempting to give other clues that reflect the emotion in the situation ☺.

As there are many people to communicate with on a typical project, the project manager should prepare a **communication plan**. The communication plan typically contains details of what information is to be communicated to whom, why, when, where, how and through which medium, and the desired impact.

The communication plan brings together the APM topic of stakeholder management (topic 2.2) with communication. The methods and media for communication chosen should engage and influence key stakeholders throughout the life of the project. There are many different communication methods and media, each of which is useful in different situations. These include:

- impromptu one-to-one conversations – 'management by walking about'
- formal one-to-one meetings
- telephone conversations
- email exchanges
- written reports for formal presentation of selected information – different types of report may be required for different stakeholders
- progress meetings for communicating to a number of people simultaneously; however, to be most effective they need to be managed and have a proper agenda
- notice boards for communication of selected information
- newsletters for communication to a large group of stakeholders without any discrimination
- chat rooms on an intranet
- road shows for communication to a more widely dispersed population of stakeholders.

The method used to communicate needs to be appropriate if the message and the meaning are to get through. For example, an appropriate method of giving feedback to a team member on performance issues would be on a one-to-one basis. An inappropriate method would be to mention it at a team meeting.

None of the above can be considered to be effective without some sort of response from the recipient. It is therefore important that the project manager is available to receive responses and to listen to concerns.

Project Red Nose Day

Communication is going to prove a very important part of the RND project. If no one knows about the events that are going to take place, then you'll raise very little money and the day will be a disaster.

You will be preparing a communication plan for the project. You have already identified the following methods of communication that you will use:

- formal one-to-one meetings with the sponsor and other key stakeholders, such as the managing director
- daily telephone conversations with team members
- email exchanges to keep some stakeholders up to date on a daily basis
- progress meetings for communicating to the whole project team – you intend to hold these on a weekly basis
- notice boards for communication of event information to all the staff in head office
- the company newsletter for communication to the whole company – you believe that this may enable you to raise more money.

Personal reflection

Think about projects you know well and the typical methods and media used for communication with stakeholders.

How many different methods were used to communicate?

Was communication effective?

How might communication be improved?

Briefly describe your views on the importance of developing appropriate communication methods and media.

_____

_____

_____

_____

_____

_____

_____

_____

Business case 9

Topic 5.1 in the *APM Body of Knowledge* covers the ownership, purpose, content and audience for the business case. This key document sets out why the project should be undertaken. It contains all the information necessary to enable an assessment of a project proposal by an organisation's decision-makers so they can make a reasoned decision on whether to invest in the project. The business case should therefore be written following a wide-ranging assessment of the costs and benefits of the proposed project. It must provide as much information as necessary to enable the decision-making process.

DEFINE THE OWNERSHIP OF A BUSINESS CASE

The sponsor owns the business case and it is their responsibility to ensure that it is developed and produced. They may delegate this task to the project manager or other members of the project team to write the document on their behalf. The business case must be formally approved by the sponsor but may also have other signatories from the steering group (project board). Once the business case is approved the project can proceed to the more detailed planning or definition phase and the preparation of the project management plan (PMP), which is described in the next chapter.

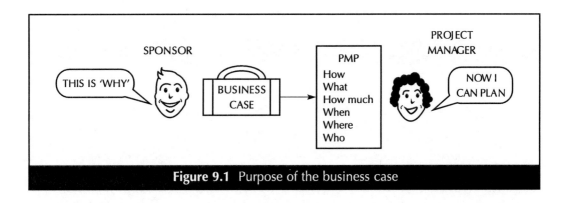

Figure 9.1 Purpose of the business case

DEFINE THE PURPOSE AND CONTENT OF THE BUSINESS CASE

The business case summarises the rationale of 'why' the project should be considered and the forecasted benefits that will come from its successful completion. Because the business case justifies the investment in the project on behalf of the organisation it will often contain financial figures relating to:

■ costs of implementing the project
■ ongoing costs relating to the operation of the deliverables (if appropriate)
■ income expected after the successful delivery of the project.

A business case will also contain a statement of the project's cost, time and quality objectives, as well as other relevant success criteria. Assumptions being made by project stakeholders should be included along with known constraints and issues, and the first attempt at identifying threats and opportunities (risks). In many cases there are a number of different ways that an organisation could achieve the same or similar objectives. Where options have been considered they are also referred to in the business case so the organisation has a historical record of why a particular approach was chosen.

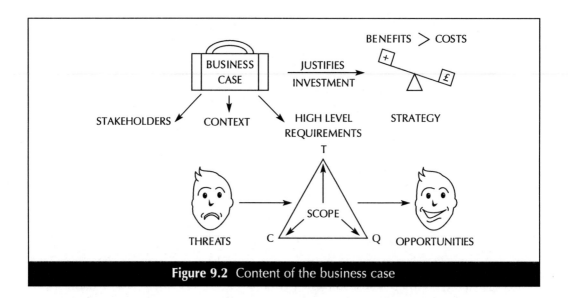

Figure 9.2 Content of the business case

A business case is most often presented as a text document using a series of standard headings. Alternatively, for a smaller project, a business case might be just a short statement with very little formal structure.

For example, in order to meet government legislation, the company needs to review and revise all of its policies relating to the hiring and firing of staff. The work must be completed by 31 March 2009. It must be in accordance with the relevant quality standards and current employee legislation. Failure to meet the required completion date will leave the company open to a substantial fine and damage to its reputation. In such a situation there is no financial justification performed, or options analysed. The project is a 'must-do', or compliance project, for the organisation.

The business case should always be referred to throughout the project, especially during the change control process. The project team must be able to validate and confirm that the business case can still be met at all times.

Project Red Nose Day

The business case for the local RND project at its simplest level is based upon a judgement that the benefits to the national charity, combined with the opportunity for staff to be socially involved and the company to be seen as supportive, outweigh the costs to the organisation in terms of direct and indirect costs.

The following success criteria summarise the business case:

- the project is a workplace event and should involve as many people as possible
- It must take place in exactly ten weeks' time, and all the money donated should be received or collected within four weeks of the close of the event
- it must utilise no more than 1000 hours of company time, and require no more than an additional £500 of company expenditure
- it should aim to raise £10,000 for a range of charitable causes approved and supported by participating staff and the charity coordinating the national link-up to this event, Comic Relief
- there should be no complaints from staff about the events
- there should be no complaints from customers about reduced service as a result of staff participation in the events
- the company should get good press through local newspaper, radio and TV coverage
- when questioned after RND, 90% of staff will support an RND project next year.

Personal reflection

Think of a number of projects at work that have involved your department.

Was the rationale for the business undertaking in each project similar – for example, to deliver a product or service to an external client, or to improve internal efficiency?

Briefly describe what you believe to be the key reasons for the projects you are familiar with, i.e. why do you think they have been approved?

What benefits are/were anticipated?

Have you seen the business case for the project?

Briefly describe how you believe your organisation manages this part of the project life cycle and suggest how it could be improved.

_____

_____

_____

_____

_____

_____

_____

_____

_____

Project management plan 10

Topic 2.4 of the *APM Body of Knowledge* covers the purpose, ownership, content, benefits and audience for a document known as the project management plan (PMP). This document takes forward the business case and details all the outcomes from the planning process, providing the essential reference for managing the project throughout its life cycle. The PMP does not need to be a big or complicated document, but it must outline the way in which the project will be taken forward in a way that all stakeholders can understand.

DEFINE THE PURPOSE, CONTENT AND BENEFITS OF A PROJECT MANAGEMENT PLAN (PMP)

The **purpose** of the PMP is to document *how* the project will be done, *when* it will take place, *where* the work will be carried out and *who* will do the work. Add to this a statement of *why* the project is taking place, summarised from the business case, *what* the project will deliver and *how much* it will cost, then what has been produced is the **project management plan (PMP)**. Another term used is a *project initiation document* or *PID*, but the abbreviation PMP will be used throughout this book.

The PMP is produced during the definition phase of the project. It is the organisation's prime mechanism for giving its formal go-ahead for the project, based on plans to do all the work that is necessary to achieve the specific objectives for change.

The PMP is not a static or fixed document. When the project is formally approved at the end of the definition phase, the PMP becomes the *baseline** from which progress can be monitored and subsequent changes can be controlled. It is part of the project manager's job to maintain the PMP and keep it up to date throughout the life of the project.

The **benefits** of defining the PMP and keeping it up to date are primarily related to clarity of information. With a PMP in place, at any point team members will have all the information they need to understand the project and the work they need to do. This is particularly useful when things change, for example if there is a new member of the team. Another way of considering the PMP is as the contract between the project manager and their team and the sponsor. In this way the PMP is clearly a response to the business case and everyone is clear about all aspects of how the project will meet the success criteria.

---

* Baseline – the reference levels against which the project is monitored and controlled.

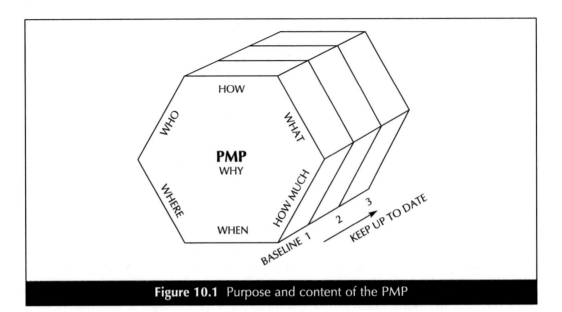

Figure 10.1 Purpose and content of the PMP

Project Red Nose Day

Before starting your RND project it would be wise to consider and document the following:

Why are you carrying out the project?	Because it is in support of a national charity that you feel strongly about. It will also be a very good social event for the company.
How will you do it?	By running fund-raising events at work on the designated Red Nose day.
What are you going to do?	Consult with staff, design the events to take place, communicate, run the 'day' itself and collect donations.
How much will it cost?	There will be no more than £500 external expenditure, but company resources such as photocopy consumables will be used free. It will also require no more than 1000 hours of staff time, which is being donated at no charge to the project.
When are you going to do the work?	Over the next ten weeks, meeting a number of *milestones** on the way.

---

* Milestone – a key event selected for its importance in the project. Note: milestones are commonly used in relation to progress. They are often chosen to represent the start of a new phase or completion of a major deliverable, and are used to monitor progress at summary level.

Where are you going to do it?	Wholly within the company's head office.
Who will do the work?	You and other corporate resources including legal, reprographics and HR.

The points in the list cover the contents of a PMP. It should be obvious why it is best to consider each of these points before spending any money or a lot of time on the project. It would be far better to know before you start if you cannot have free access to photocopier consumables so that you can make alternative arrangements. The PMP needs further work before it is a working plan that can be formally agreed between you and the sponsor, but this is a start.

Personal reflection

Think about a project you know well and the project management plan that was produced.

Did the PMP answer the following questions:

- why?
- how?
- what?
- how much?
- when?
- where?
- who?

Was the PMP kept up to date as the project progressed?

Write a short description of how the PMP might have been used to better effect for the project. What was missing from the PMP?

_____

_____

_____

_____

_____

_____

_____

_____

_____

DEFINE THE OWNERSHIP OF A PMP

The project management plan (PMP) is owned by the project manager, which means that she is accountable for its creation and for keeping it up to date. However, a project manager may be very busy or not have all the right skills to produce all the contents of the PMP, and may rely on other project team members to produce parts of it.

The PMP should be agreed and signed off by both the project manager and sponsor as a minimum. The joint signatures of the project manager and sponsor will form a sort of contract between them, removing any doubt about what the project will deliver and to what objectives.

The PMP should be read, understood and, where appropriate, agreed to by everyone who has a significant involvement in the project. Who these people are will vary considerably depending on the nature of the project, but they will certainly include the resource managers of those involved in doing the project work and other key stakeholders.

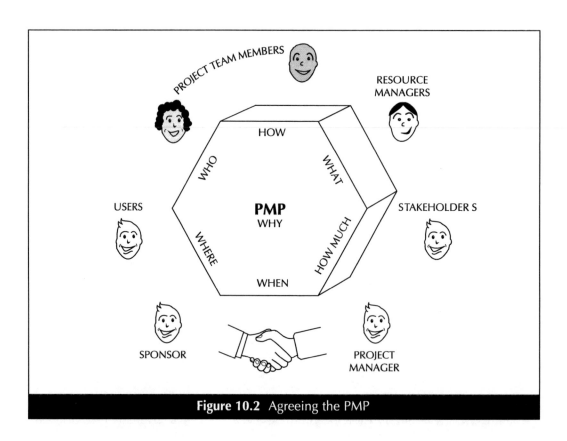

Figure 10.2 Agreeing the PMP

Project Red Nose Day

You are accountable for the project management plan for the RND project. Only if the document you prepare, in whatever format, has been read and understood by all those involved (primarily your project team, including the sponsor) can you avoid disagreements later over what you intended to do, when you intended to do it and the assistance you needed.

Personal reflection

Think about a project you know well and the project management plan that was produced.

Was the project team involved in preparing the PMP?

Briefly describe how the PMP was used as a communication tool with the project team and wider stakeholders during the course of the project.

_____

_____

_____

_____

_____

_____

_____

_____

_____

11 Scope management

Topic 3.1 in the *APM Body of Knowledge* deals with project scope and scope management, and the use of a variety of tools to define and communicate the work to be done as part of the project. The scope of the project is central, as can be seen by its position in the middle of the project manager's 'trilemma'. This makes the task of defining and managing project scope extremely important as the basis for the other planning processes that follow.

DEFINE PROJECT SCOPE AND SCOPE MANAGEMENT

A project's **scope** is the sum of the work content of a project – in other words, all the things that need to be done in order to achieve the project's time, cost and quality objectives and success criteria.

It is important that a project manager has a clear understanding of the initial scope of the project and that this understanding is communicated to the team and all stakeholders. Any subsequent changes can then be managed, and 'scope creep' can be avoided. When thinking about the scope for a project it is wise to consider not only the things that need to be done, but also the things that will not be done. This helps to remove any possible ambiguity about the project deliverables. For example, the scope of the project might be to design, build and construct a new extension for a client's house, including all electrical and plumbing work, but might exclude obtaining planning permission as well as painting and decorating. By stating that the project will not seek planning permission, the client will avoid making a potentially catastrophic assumption about the work to be undertaken on their behalf.

A project's scope is directly linked to specified time, cost and quality objectives. As already mentioned, the area inside the project management triangle (see Figure 1.4) also represents the project scope. The greater the scope, the longer a project will take and the more it will cost. When it comes to quality (or performance) the link is potentially confusing but very important.

Any reduction in scope may affect the ultimate quality of the project and mean that success criteria may not be achieved. However, this should not happen if the project manager and sponsor have a good understanding of the relative priorities of time, cost and quality.

For example, in order to keep to budget and timescale, a manager in an office refurbishment project may decide not to soundproof the partition walls in meeting rooms. This could be seen as a reduction in scope for the project. As a result of this decision, staff might avoid the rooms to preserve confidentiality and instead hire hotel space for important meetings, and at a significant cost to the organisation each month. As an alternative, the project team might decide to reduce the quality/performance criteria of the soundproofing in the project plan. By reducing the specification of the soundproofing it may be possible to achieve the time and cost objectives and also to produce a product that is fit for purpose.

The project manager must decide whether to keep the original scope and quality in the plan or spend more money and/or take more time. Whatever is decided, the relationship between the scope and the project's objectives should always be clear.

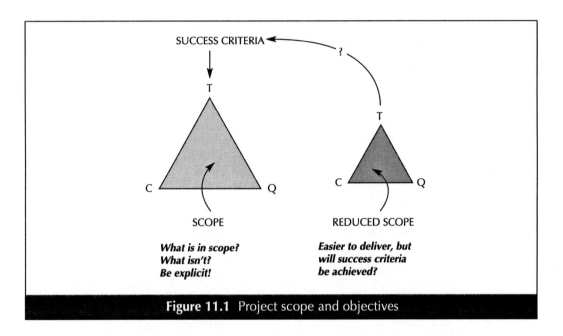

Figure 11.1 Project scope and objectives

Scope management involves identifying and defining all the elements of the project scope, and for keeping the scope current at all times with a clear definition of what is in scope and what is out. Scope creep is a major problem on some projects, and the project manager protects the scope, or changes it only after proper review, using a change control process as described in Chapter 20.

Project Red Nose Day

The success criteria for this project have been defined in these terms:

- the RND project is a workplace event and should involve as many people as possible
- it must take place in exactly ten weeks' time, and all the money donated should be received or collected within four weeks of the close of the event
- it must utilise no more than 1000 hours of company time, and require no more than an additional £500 of company expenditure

- it should aim to raise £10,000 for a range of charitable causes approved and supported by participating staff and the charity coordinating the national link-up to this event, Comic Relief
- there should be no complaints from staff about the events
- there should be no complaints from customers about reduced service as a result of staff participation in the events
- the company should get good press through local newspaper, radio and TV coverage
- when questioned after RND, 90% of staff will support an RND project next year.

The scope of the project is to do all the things necessary to achieve the project's objectives. One key aspect of the scope to be defined is the number of different events you will have that will balance the need for maximum involvement of staff within the budget. You and your team believe that the right number of events to host is three if the objectives and success criteria as defined above are to be met.

If any of the project's objectives were changed this would have a direct influence on the project's scope. It is extremely unlikely that the date for Red Nose Day will be changed, but any change in the date would cause havoc with the project's objectives. If the sponsor decides to reduce the amount of free company time available to, say, 500 hours, this would certainly mean that holding three events would no longer be viable. This would, in turn, mean that raising £10,000 would be less likely.

Personal reflection

Think about a project you know well.

Think about how the scope of the project is inextricably linked to the project's time, cost and quality objectives.

Briefly describe some examples from your experience that show how important it is to define the scope fully and completely – understanding equally what is out of scope and what is in scope.

_____

_____

_____

_____

_____

_____

_____

_____

DEFINE THE MAIN BREAKDOWN STRUCTURES USED FOR PRODUCT, WORK, COST AND ORGANISATION (PBS, WBS, CBS AND OBS)

Project managers use breakdown structures to literally break down or decompose the project into more detailed parts. They provide an essential structure for project planning, monitoring and control. There are four primary breakdown structures that are used during core project planning.

The **product breakdown structure (PBS)** is a hierarchy of products (another term for deliverables) that are required to be produced to complete the project. A PBS uses nouns (names of deliverables at various levels). The lowest level of a PBS is a project deliverable.

The **work breakdown structure (WBS)** is slightly different in that it is a hierarchy that leads to the work that needs to be done to complete the project. A WBS uses verbs and nouns (things that need to be done at various levels). The lowest level of a WBS is either called a *work package** or an activity.

One commonly used approach to define project scope is to start with a PBS to identify the main products, then at a certain level of definition further break down the products into packages of **work** that can be assigned to project team members to perform. This combined technique can be the most useful way of ensuring that all the deliverables to be produced and all the work to be done are captured.

Whatever technique is used (PBS, WBS or combined PBS/WBS), the objective is to define the scope of the project completely and in sufficient detail so that team members can do the work. It is particularly important when considering if ALL the work has been defined to include all the management work and products as well as all the technical work and specialist products.

Irrespective of the technique used, each 'box' in the breakdown structure should be uniquely identified with a code. An example is shown in Figure 11.2.

The **cost breakdown structure (CBS)** also represents the work of the project but this time organised as a hierarchical breakdown of cost elements. This is of particular use when organising budgets and allocating expenditure for work in a way that can be dealt with and reported in a sensible way by the management accountants.

The **organisational breakdown structure (OBS)** also represents the work of the project but this time organised as a hierarchical breakdown of the management groups and resources involved in the project. An OBS often resembles an organisation chart and shows the project organisation in enough detail for work to be allocated to groups, units or individuals.

Both the CBS and OBS increase in complexity depending on the number of levels that are defined in the original PBS, WBS or combined PBS/WBS.

---

* Work package – a group of related activities that are defined at the same level within a work breakdown structure.

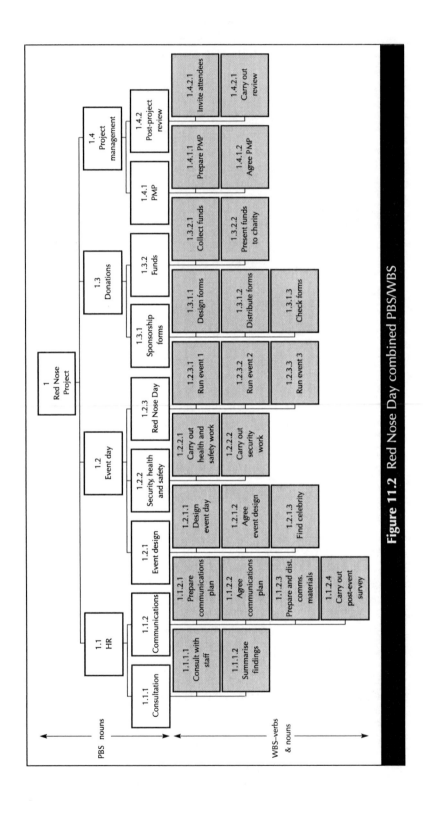

Figure 11.2 Red Nose Day combined PBS/WBS

Project Red Nose Day

The breakdown structure in Figure 11.2 is a combined PBS and WBS for the RND project. The boxes with the white background are the project's products or deliverables and the boxes with the shaded backgrounds are the project's activities or work packages.

Personal reflection

Think about a project that is just about to start, either in your workplace or in a social context.

Consider how you could use the breakdown structures outlined (PBS, WBS, CBS and OBS) to aid the planning of the project.

Sketch a product breakdown structure that separates into simpler constituent parts (i.e. decomposes) the scope of this project to a third level (as described) using just nouns; then decompose the structure a step further, using verbs and nouns, and use this exercise to describe some level 4 work packages.

_____

_____

_____

_____

_____

_____

_____

_____

_____

_____

DEFINE THE PURPOSE AND USE OF A RESPONSIBILITY
ASSIGNMENT MATRIX (RAM)

All projects involve more than one person, or the work would simply be a routine task. Most projects involve tens of different people, many of whom are from different departments, functions or even organisations, such as suppliers or contractors or external regulatory bodies. In the world of project management, the sponsor is accountable for delivering the business benefits and the project manager is accountable for delivering the project as agreed in the PMP according to its time, cost and quality objectives. Being accountable, however, doesn't mean that either the sponsor or the project manager has sole responsibility for doing the work.

A **responsibility assignment matrix or RAM** is used to define who in the organisation of the project is responsible for each of the project's deliverables. It is a grid along two dimensions which combines the project's work breakdown structure (or product breakdown structure) along one axis, with its organisation breakdown structure along the other axis. In each cell of the grid (see Figure 11.3) a coding structure is used to determine the relative involvement of each party in each product or piece of work.

A typical coding system might be:

- R – Responsible
- A – Accountable (or Approval)
- C – Consult
- I – Inform.

An example using the above coding might be the project's end of project report. The project manager is *accountable* for this. They may choose to delegate this *responsibility* to the project office, who in turn will *consult* with the sponsor and other stakeholders when preparing it. All other team members will be *informed* of the outcome. Some organisations use other coding structures that may relate to a particular function: for example, in engineering D might be used for design, C for checking and I for inspection.

The purpose of a responsibility assignment matrix is to ensure that all members of the team are aware of their responsibilities and how they fit into the broader picture of the project. It will also avoid the risk that no one takes total responsibility for certain products or work, or that key consultations or checks are missed.

PBS or WBS		Sponsor	Project manager	Health and safety officer	Security adviser	Event 1 manager	Event 2 manager	Event 3 manager	Finance manager	Quality manager
	Consultation	R	A/R	I	I	C	C	C	I	C
	Communication	C	A/R	C	C	C	C	C	I	C
	Event design	C	A	C	C	R	R	R	I	C
	Health and safety	I	A	R	C	C	C	C	I	C
	Security	I	A	C	R	C	C	C	I	C
	Red Nose Day	A	R	C	C	R	R	R	I	I
	Sponsorship forms	C	A/R	I	I	C	C	C	C	C
	Funds	A	C	I	I	I	I	I	R	I
	PMP	C	A/R	C	C	C	C	C	C	C
	Post-project review	C	A/R	C	C	C	C	C	C	C

Figure 11.3 Responsibility assignment matrix

Project Red Nose Day

There are a number of key accountabilities and responsibilities on the project which are highlighted in the responsibility assignment matrix in Figure 11.3.

Personal reflection

Think about the times that you have seen a RAM – often called a RACI chart – used in practice. If you have never seen one, select a role from the illustration in Figure 11.3 and reflect on the responsibilities allocated to that individual.

Sketch a simple RAM for a project you know well and briefly describe the advantages you think would result from producing such a document.

_____

_____

_____

_____

_____

_____

_____

_____

_____

12 Project quality management

Topic 2.6 in the *APM Body of Knowledge* deals with project quality and project quality management, and defines the differences between quality planning, quality assurance and quality control. Quality forms one of the dimensions of the time, cost and quality triangle and as such needs to be rigorously and proactively managed. There is no point in delivering something on time and to budget that nobody wants, likes or can use!

DEFINE QUALITY AND QUALITY MANAGEMENT

The most common way of defining the **quality** of a deliverable or product is to say that it must be 'fit for purpose'. This means that it meets the stated requirements – no more, no less. Quality is not about 'doing the best you can' or 'excellence' in any way. It is about defining the standards that need to be achieved and then doing it – reliably and consistently.

Project quality management is the discipline applied to all work that is done to make sure that the deliverables from projects are fit for purpose.

Deliverables from projects will include:

- products or services, such as a mobile telephone made to a new design or a management report from the definition phase of the project
- records that provide evidence of how the project management processes were managed, such as the project's business case, the PMP, risk log etc. – these deliverables are often called 'management products'.

It is a fact that the standard that is achieved for every deliverable will be of concern to at least one stakeholder. Achieving stakeholder requirements is the principle that drives the project quality management process. When requirements are understood, acceptance criteria can be developed for each deliverable or product. With acceptance criteria in place, plans can be made to ensure that results are achieved and can be proven.

You will notice that project quality management is not about compliance with quality management standards such as ISO 9000 : 2000. Such a standard is a good way for an organisation to control processes, and the project management process for your organisation may be controlled using such a system. Compliance with ISO 9000 must not be confused with project quality management, which is about ensuring that specific deliverables meet specific objectives for change.

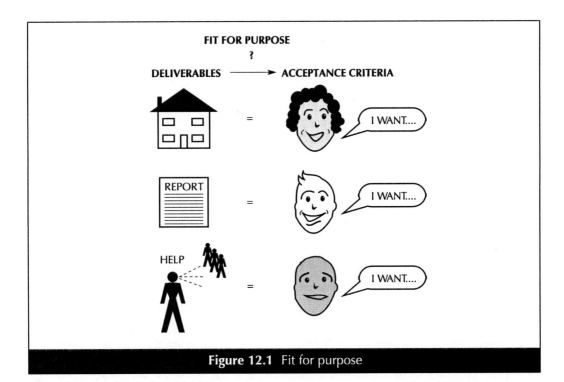

Figure 12.1 Fit for purpose

Project Red Nose Day

There are many deliverables from the RND project that need to be fit for purpose. Three examples are:

1 Fundraising events to take place on National *Red Nose Day* in your offices, although note that the number of events has not yet been finalised
2 Correctly completed sponsorship forms
3 An agreed plan for the day.

Acceptance criteria for these three deliverables have been agreed as follows:

1 The organisation and delivery of each event must actively involve ten people to organise and run the event, and attract a minimum of 200 other staff to attend. Each event must take place safely and without upsetting anyone, and cater for staff with physical disabilities.
2 All sponsorship forms should contain the sponsoring person's name, department or address and telephone number, and a clear statement of the amount donated. All writing should be in ink and must be legible.
3 An agreed plan for the day, including a schedule of events, must be prepared and agreed by the sponsor and project team within six weeks.

Personal reflection

Think about a project that you know well.

Think about the deliverables from the project (they could have alternatively been called products).

How was quality defined for those deliverables?

Briefly describe how the project quality management process made sure that stakeholder requirements were met.

✎ _____

_____

_____

_____

_____

_____

_____

_____

_____

_____

DEFINE THE DIFFERENCES BETWEEN QUALITY PLANNING, QUALITY ASSURANCE AND QUALITY CONTROL

To achieve project quality management, three basic techniques need to be used.

Quality planning is the process for determining which quality standards are applicable to the project and how to apply them. Quality standards may relate to the industry sector, for example compliance with QS 9000 in the automotive sector. They may also apply to the organisation, i.e. compulsory company standards or quality policy, or to a client organisation, i.e. to supply to the client evidence of control to ISO 9000. Once the standards are understood, plans to achieve them must be made and documented in a quality plan which is a key part of the project management plan (PMP).

Some organisations treat specific health, safety and environmental standards as inputs to the quality planning process: this is good practice.

Quality assurance is needed to evaluate the overall project performance on a periodic basis to provide confidence that the process is effective and that objectives will be met. The principal way of achieving this is through periodic quality audits, using people independent of the project delivery team to check that processes and ways of working meet stated requirements. Specific work results are not checked as part of quality assurance: the purpose is to review whether the underlying processes and ways of working are leading towards product deliverables of the right quality. The project manager must then consider and action the recommendations made by the auditor. This role is often performed by a part of the project organisation called 'project assurance'.

The strategy for quality assurance is typically described in the quality plan section of the PMP for the project, e.g. to outline who will conduct audits, to what scope, when and where.

Quality control verifies that the specific project deliverables comply with the quality standards outlined in the quality plan and the acceptance criteria for the deliverables. Quality control may be achieved by physically inspecting or checking particular items: for instance, peer review of design calculations or a piece of marketing literature. Alternatively it can be achieved through surveying a group of people: e.g. to find out if employees are satisfied following a reorganisation, a questionnaire-type method could be used.

A key part of quality management associated with quality control is to find out the causes of any errors or problems and to address these so they don't happen again. This approach leads to *continuous improvement* *.

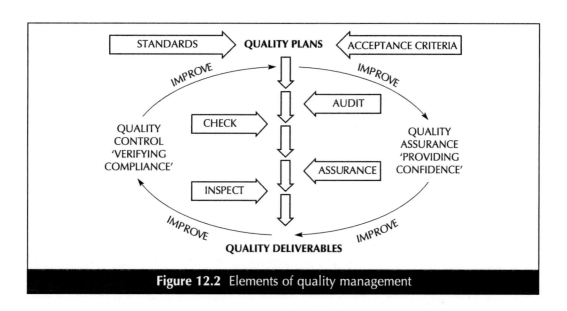

Figure 12.2 Elements of quality management

---

* Continuous improvement – the culture and planned systematic approach to improvement that needs to be created to ensure that lessons are learned, and that the root causes of problems are identified and managed so that the same mistake is never made on more than one occasion.

Project Red Nose Day

As part of your planning for the RND project you need to involve the company's health and safety officer when designing the events. You will ask him to make sure that each event can be carried out safely and be prepared to accept his recommendations for any changes. You have also arranged to meet him on a weekly basis to review all aspects of the project.

To check that the sponsorship forms are being filled in correctly you have asked each of your team to carry out random reviews of forms being used within their departments. If they find any forms that are poorly completed they will encourage the form owner to correct the deficiency.

Personal reflection

Think about a project you know well.

Consider the explanations given for quality planning, quality assurance and quality control. Can you see if and how each was applied on the project?

Briefly describe good practice and areas for improvement from your experience in this area.

_____

_____

_____

_____

_____

_____

_____

_____

_____

Estimating 13

Topic 4.3 in the *APM Body of Knowledge* deals with estimating and looks at three primary estimating methods and the concept of the estimating funnel. Some say that project plans are in effect 'educated guesses' based on an assessment of what work needs to be done and estimates of how long that work might take to do and how much it might cost. It follows then that anything that can be done to improve estimates and make guesses as 'educated as practically possible' is worth the effort.

DEFINE WHAT AN ESTIMATE IS AND THE CONCEPT OF THE ESTIMATING FUNNEL

An ***estimate*** is a quantified approximation of project costs, durations and resources. Estimates are necessary for all projects. Without estimates you cannot put together a schedule, establish resource needs or draw up a budget. An estimate can never be 100% accurate, unless you are extremely lucky, and so it is best not to refer to accuracy and estimate in the same phrase. We will refer to the range of an estimate, i.e. the breadth of tolerance around the expected result.

Estimating is most difficult at the start of the project when there is lots of uncertainty about what is to be done, when, by whom etc. An estimate prepared at the beginning of the project is likely to have a wide range when compared to an estimate prepared during the last phases of a project when the detail of the project is more clearly understood.

It is quite normal to update estimates throughout the life cycle of the project. Perhaps the most important estimate is the one that accompanies the project management plan (PMP). This is because it is this estimate upon which the project will be authorised. Many organisations look for an estimate that has a range of only plus or minus 10% at this point.

This idea that estimates improve as the project progresses through the life cycle is often called the ***estimating funnel***.

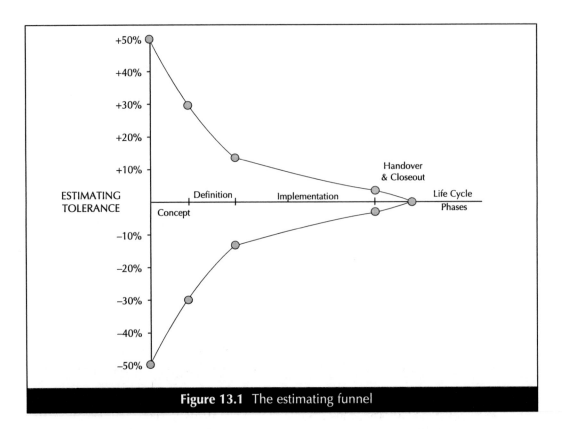

Figure 13.1 The estimating funnel

Project Red Nose Day

You have put together initial plans for the project but haven't completed work on the project management plan (PMP). The plans so far contain a number of estimates particularly relating to the duration of project activities and the amount of effort (primarily yours) that will be required. These original estimates will be refined as part of the preparation of the Red Nose Day PMP.

It will not be possible to come up with a definitive estimate until after the individual events have been designed, which is five weeks into the project.

Personal reflection

Think about projects you know well, either at work or at home.

Consider the difficulties of estimating durations, resources needed and costs, and the impact of being wrong, given that all project plans are put together using these 'guesses'.

Briefly describe the methods you personally have used, or have seen used, to put together estimates for the project.

_____

_____

_____

_____

_____

_____

_____

_____

DEFINE THE THREE PRIMARY ESTIMATING METHODS

The only technique that can be used if the organisation has no experience of doing a project like the one being estimated is to use ***bottom-up estimating***. This requires the preparation of a work breakdown structure (WBS) for the project down to a level of detail that allows a cost to be estimated by the 'owner' of each work package or activity. The individual estimates are then summed to give the total estimate for the project.

Bottom-up estimating takes time, whereas ***comparative estimating*** is relatively quick if the organisation has some relevant past experience. To prepare a comparative estimate, the current project is compared to others like it, while at the same time asking questions such as:

- Is it bigger or smaller than the ones we are comparing to?
- Is it more or less complex?
- Is it using the same technology or design methods?

Using this approach, the answer might be that it is twice as big as the last similar project, is a little more complex and uses improved design methods. Therefore the answer chosen might be to double the cost of the last project to create the estimate for the new project.

Another method of estimating if the organisation has data from past similar projects relies on the use of key parameters or measures and is known as ***parametric estimating***. The parameters are fed into a model to create an estimate. Examples of parametric estimating are often found in the IT industry. Typical parameters might be the number of data entry screens to be prepared, or the number of reports to be prepared. If values for these parameters, as well as a few others, are fed into a model, it will then generate an estimate of how much effort is required to complete the work. Parametric estimating requires an organisation to hold a considerable amount of historic data and to keep it up to date.

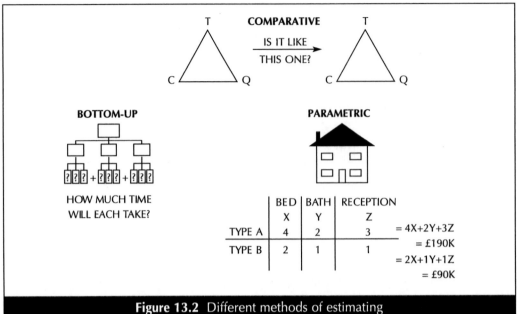

Figure 13.2 Different methods of estimating

Project Red Nose Day

You have never worked on a project like this before but the combined PBS/WBS you have developed has allowed you to carry out bottom-up estimating.

The lack of experience means that there is no data to carry out a comparative or parametric estimate. At least in the future, should the company want to do something similar, the data from this project will allow an overall comparative estimate to be used at the start and for parametric estimates to be established for key aspects of the project. Examples might be the amount of staff time used in ratio to the number of events, or the ratio between the number of events and the amount of money raised.

Personal reflection

From your previous reflection on the methods you have experienced for putting together project estimates, how do they compare to the ones listed?

Briefly describe how the terms used for the three types of estimate compare to your everyday experience.

14 Scheduling

Topic 3.2 in the *APM Body of Knowledge* deals with the purpose and key aspects of scheduling, which means planning when activities will be carried out. Understanding scheduling involves learning the definitions of network diagram, Gantt (bar) chart, critical path, total float, free float, milestones and baseline. The ideas underpinning scheduling are often seen as being at the centre of project management. As a result people are often lulled into thinking that the first thing they must do is put together the schedule using commonly available computer software. The fact is that proper scheduling is a major help when managing a project, but proper schedules can be put together only when all the other things previously covered in this book are already in place.

Readers using this book to study for the APM Introductory Certificate in Project Management should note that the concept of free float is not included in the syllabus: however, understanding this concept will considerably enhance understanding of scheduling, hence its inclusion in this chapter.

DEFINE SCHEDULING, CRITICAL PATH, TOTAL FLOAT, FREE FLOAT AND THE USE OF THE GANTT (BAR) CHART

When a project manager has defined the scope of the project and the activities that need to be completed, and has estimates of activity durations in place, the next step is to put together a schedule. This **scheduling** enables the project manager to predict the overall project duration and when activities and events are planned to happen.

To move from a list of activities with estimates to a schedule the project manager needs to do two more things. First, identify logical dependencies between activities to determine the order, or sequence, in which those activities need to be carried out. A logical dependency identifies predecessors and successors for activities. Typical dependencies used are:

- finish to start (activity A must finish before activity B starts)
- start to start (activity B can only start when activity A has started)
- finish to finish (activity B can only finish when activity A has finished).

Second, the project manager needs to identify resource requirements and availability (this will be dealt with in full in Chapter 15).

The scope, estimates, logical dependencies and understanding of resource requirements together mean that the project manager can now define the sequence of work through the project. All this information is used to prepare the project network, which can be done either by hand or using a computer-based tool. Figure 14.1 is a drawing of a network for the RND project. The numbers for activities relate to the names for the same activities in Figure 14.2

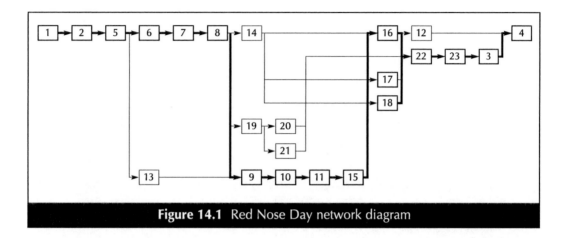

Figure 14.1 Red Nose Day network diagram

The network diagram enables the project manager to identify the critical path or paths for the project.

Critical path is a term that is synonymous with project management. All projects have a critical path, and some have more than one. A critical path will determine the shortest time in which a project can be completed. Another way of expressing this is to say that the critical path also represents the longest path of activity through the project. Both of these statements describe the significance of a critical path.

The purpose of a project manager understanding a project's critical path(s) is to be able to focus effort in managing the activities that lie on it with the knowledge that if all of them complete on time, and if there is no slippage on other activities that exceeds the *total float**, the whole project will finish on time.

The most common way of showing a project's schedule is to use a **Gantt (bar) chart** as it is relatively simple to read and understand. A Gantt chart can be as simple as a list of activities drawn against a horizontal timescale, with each activity represented by a bar that also shows the period over which it is to be carried out.

Until the mid-1970s project scheduling was something that was done by a person by hand, using mental arithmetic. Changing the information once drawn was time-consuming. There are now various software tools that use a graphical user interface (GUI) to do the drawing and the maths, and will plot the schedule information in many formats. Computer software is not needed to prepare schedules but it can be very useful.

The information contained within a project network diagram or a Gantt chart for a project is the same: they are just different means of displaying the same information.

---

* Total float – time by which an activity may be delayed or extended without affecting the total project duration.

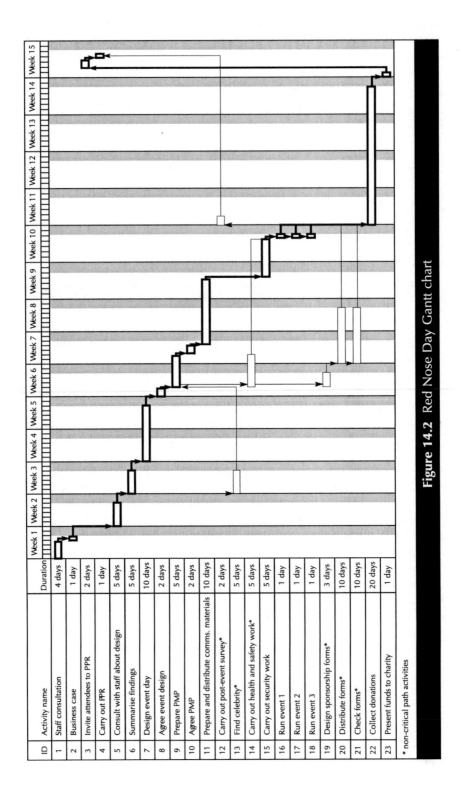

ID	Activity name	Duration
1	Staff consultation	4 days
2	Business case	1 day
3	Invite attendees to PPR	2 days
4	Carry out PPR	1 day
5	Consult with staff about design	5 days
6	Summarise findings	5 days
7	Design event day	10 days
8	Agree event design	2 days
9	Prepare PMP	5 days
10	Agree PMP	2 days
11	Prepare and distribute comms. materials	10 days
12	Carry out post-event survey*	2 days
13	Find celebrity*	5 days
14	Carry out health and safety work*	5 days
15	Carry out event security work	5 days
16	Run event 1	1 day
17	Run event 2	1 day
18	Run event 3	1 day
19	Design sponsorship forms*	3 days
20	Distribute forms*	10 days
21	Check forms*	10 days
22	Collect donations	20 days
23	Present funds to charity	1 day

* non-critical path activities

Figure 14.2 Red Nose Day Gantt chart

Clearly not all activities are on the critical path for a project. The ones that are not on the critical path have what is officially described as float (in the UK) or slack (in the USA). There are two different kinds of float – total float, as previously mentioned, and *free float**. Both total and free float relate to the amount of leeway there is in relation to when an activity needs to take place in order to maintain the overall project schedule.

A project manager who understands which activities in their project have float and which are critical will be better able to make decisions relating to whether the start of an activity can be delayed or not.

For example, consider a project that has three sequential activities, A, B and C, that all have finish-to-start dependencies. Activity A has five days' total float and zero free float, B has five days' total float and five days' free float and C has zero total float and free float. With this information the project manager knows that if the finish of A is delayed by three days, the owner of activity B will need to be warned that the start of their work will be delayed by three days. The project manager can still rest easy, though, as the overall project completion date will remain unaffected as A has five days' total float. Assume now that A doesn't get delayed but, for whatever reason, it would benefit the project to delay the start and finish of B by five days. Because B has five days' free float the project manager knows that the effect of this does not need to be discussed with any other activity owner. As long as the finish of B is not delayed more than five days the start of C is unaffected.

Another example of total float and free float is shown in Figure 14.3 for the RND project. From this you should be able to see that activity 19, 'Design sponsorship forms', has a total float of ten days but has zero free float because any delay in its completion will delay the start of activity 20, 'Distribute forms'. Activity 20 has ten days' total float and ten days' free float. This means that its completion can be delayed by up to ten days before it delays the whole project.

Once the schedule has been fully developed and included in the PMP, it is said to be 'baselined'. The baseline is the version of the schedule against which the project's time objectives will be monitored and controlled. The concept of the baseline applies equally to all aspects of the PMP, not just the schedule.

Project Red Nose Day

Figures 14.1 and 14.2 illustrate the RND project schedule shown as a network diagram and Gantt chart respectively. Note that the critical path is highlighted in bold. The boxes represent activities.

Figure 14.3 shows the difference between total float and free float for the RND project.

---

* Free float – time by which an activity may be delayed or extended without affecting the start of any succeeding activity.

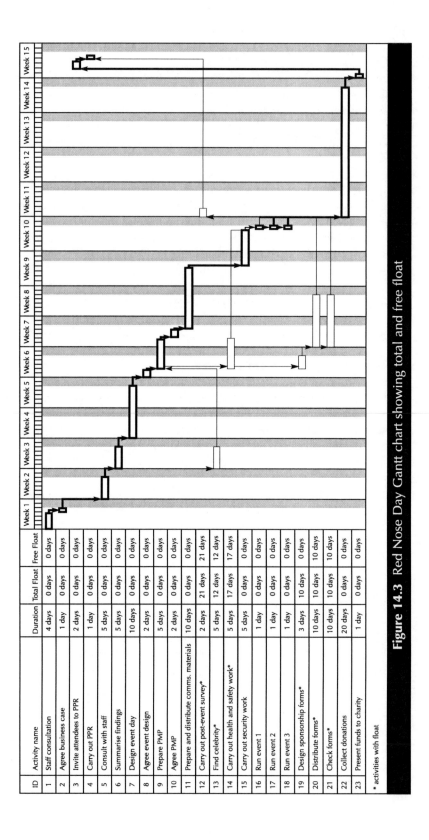

Figure 14.3 Red Nose Day Gantt chart showing total and free float

Personal reflection

Think about a project you know well.

Were you aware of the concept of the critical path and how the project manager worked to protect the activities on the critical path so that the overall timescale for the project did not slip?

Were you aware which activities had float and what this meant for the importance of the timing of those activities?

Briefly outline two things in your own words:

- what the critical path for the project represents and why it is important to understand it
- the importance of understanding the amount of total float and free float on activities.

Consider how it is necessary to have completed a work breakdown structure to decompose the project scope before you can begin to create the project schedule.

_____

_____

_____

_____

_____

_____

_____

_____

_____

DEFINE MILESTONE

In preparing project schedules another key technique is the use of **milestones**. As the name suggests, milestones indicate key points in the schedule. Milestones represent the completion of deliverables or highlight key decision points on the project. They are not activities because they have no (zero) duration.

Milestones can simplify the communication of the schedule by reporting the status of the project at a summary level. This kind of communication is essential for senior management or other parties who may not necessarily be interested in the detail of the project, but are interested in its outcome and progress.

Milestones can also be used to set targets and monitor progress. Rather than just having a target completion date for the end of the project, interim targets based on milestones can be established that can be monitored more closely than the multitude of activities that make up the project. Many organisations also use the completion of milestones as a means of determining when they pay their suppliers or contractors. This avoids paying for work that has not been done.

A project to design and roll out a new IT system across 30 offices might have milestones planned as follows:

- PMP signed off
- user requirements completed
- final design agreed
- pilot system tested
- final version agreed
- 10 installations complete
- 20 installations complete
- 30 installations complete.

Project Red Nose Day

The main milestones for the RND project could be as follows (see also Figure 14.4):

- business case agreed
- staff consultation complete
- event design agreed
- communications complete
- RND complete
- post-event survey complete
- sponsorship money collected.

Personal reflection

Think about a project you know well that is now complete.

Consider what milestones were set for the project and how they were used to aid planning, communication and control.

Define some appropriate milestones for a project you know of that is just being planned.

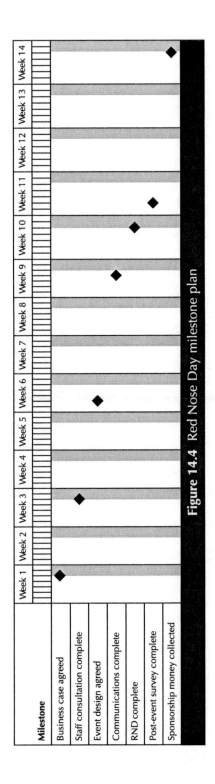

Figure 14.4 Red Nose Day milestone plan

15 Resource management

Topic 3.3 in the *APM Body of Knowledge* deals with resource management and the concepts of resource smoothing and resource levelling as ways of making sure that the work to be done on the project is done at the best possible time given the project objectives and resources available. This is another aspect of project management with particular technical language to learn, but the concepts underpinning the terms are simpler to understand than the language might suggest.

DEFINE RESOURCE MANAGEMENT, RESOURCE SMOOTHING AND RESOURCE LEVELLING

Resources, in project management terms, are people, equipment, facilities or any other entity that is needed to complete an activity and therefore costs money.

Resource management is about identifying and assigning resources to activities so that the project strikes the right balance between time taken (duration) and costs in line with the project objectives and success criteria. It is also about identifying where there are areas of the schedule that require significantly more resources than are reasonably available to the project. These resource 'peaks' need to be managed.

There is inevitably a conflict between time and cost – no one is saying 'spend as much and take as much time as you like' – so project managers need to 'optimise' resources. There are two methods used to do this.

Resource smoothing is also known as time-limited scheduling, and as the name suggests this is the process of making sure that resources are used as efficiently as possible, and of increasing or decreasing resources as required to protect the end date of the project. Using this method, time is relatively more important than cost.

Resource levelling is also known as resource-limited scheduling, and as the name suggests this is the process of making the most of the limited resources available. Resource levelling forces the amount of work scheduled not to exceed the limits of the resources available. This inevitably results in either activity durations being extended or entire activities being delayed until resource is available. Often this means a longer overall project duration. Using this method, cost is relatively more important than time.

One practical way of putting together the first iteration of a project schedule is initially to ignore the number or quantity of resources required, and the availability of these resources. The activities are sequenced and linked together graphically either using a network diagram or Gantt chart, and then resources are considered as a second step to complete the picture.

In order to understand the complete picture, the resource or resources required to work on each activity must be linked to the schedule. This might be a person's name or a skill, e.g. systems analyst or lawyer, or a company name, or a piece of equipment, such as a computer, a crane or a test rig. It is important to determine the amount of each resource that is needed. Is the resource needed on a full-time or part-time basis, and if it's part-time is it 10% or 50%, or some other percentage? Once all this level of information is established and combined with the project schedule, the resources required on any given day or in any week can be seen. This kind of information is often displayed as a resource *histogram**.

Resources (and time) are often finite, and problems arise when the resources required exceed the resources that are available to the project. A project manager might need five full-time data analysts for a crucial four-week period in the project, only to be told by the head of data analysis that there are only three available. In this case, what options are possible, assuming no more resources are actually available? In reality only two options exist and both will require the moving or rescheduling of the activities that the data analysts work on. To do this the project manager will need to know if these activities have any total float and free float.

1 The first option is to try to reschedule (in the example, the data analysts' activities) so that the need for additional resources is removed, but the end date of the project is maintained. This is the technique known as time-limited scheduling or resource smoothing. This should always be the first thing that the project manager tries, but it doesn't always work if the activities that need to be moved are either on the critical path or have insufficient total float, the result being that the peaks of resource (i.e. the times in the schedule where lots of resources are needed and you don't have them) either remain unchanged or are reduced only slightly.

2 If time-limited scheduling is unsuccessful, the only option left is to address the resource peak in the most effective and least disruptive manner. But this may result in slippage of the project's end date. This is the technique known as resource-limited scheduling or resource levelling. The sponsor may be unhappy with the resultant change to the project end date: in such a situation a potentially interesting discussion on how to resolve the problem will be needed.

---

* Histogram – a graphic display of planned and/or actual resource usage over a period of time. It is in the form of a vertical bar chart, the height of each bar representing the quantity of resource usage in a given time unit.

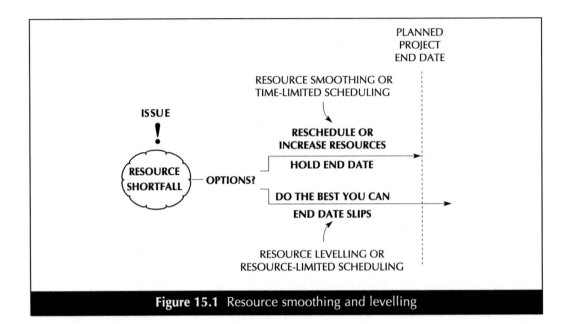

Figure 15.1 Resource smoothing and levelling

Project Red Nose Day

You are quite lucky because the RND project has very few resource issues. However, you have recognised during week 6 of the project that you yourself are working on two activities: 'prepare PMP' and 'design sponsorship forms'. You have estimated that you will need to spend 75% of your time on each of these. If this estimate proves true, then you will be overloaded. In order to avoid this you should consider rescheduling the work relating to designing sponsorship forms. Moving this work one week, i.e. within its total float, should solve your resourcing problem.

For this project, resource-limited scheduling is not possible because of the immovable end date. If resource constraints became impossible to manage, the options would be to either:

- find more resources by agreeing more company time or by securing extra funding for outside help, or
- reduce the scope of the project so less work is done.

Personal reflection

Think about a project you know well, either at work or in a domestic or social context.

Briefly outline examples where both resource smoothing (time-limited scheduling) and resource levelling (resource-limited scheduling) might be necessary. Have you ever come across a project where resources are unlimited? What do you conclude from this?

16 Teamwork and leadership

Topics 7.2 and 7.3 in the *APM Body of Knowledge* deal with teamwork and leadership within the project context. In some ways, the ideas behind teamwork and leadership are the same in all situations where people are involved because any work requires groups of people to be motivated to do that work in the best possible way. Many argue, though, that managing people in a project context requires even more of a focus on teamwork and leadership than in a business-as-usual situation. This is because there is additional stress in situations when a temporary, multidisciplinary team is brought together for a limited time to achieve objectives within time, cost and quality constraints. In such situations the project manager may have no direct authority over team members and therefore must lead through influence.

DEFINE PROJECT TEAM, TEAMWORK, TEAM BUILDING AND TEAM DEVELOPMENT

The ***project team*** is the set of individuals (groups or organisations) that is responsible to the project manager for undertaking project activities. What links them together is that they are all working together to meet a common objective, i.e. to deliver the project to its time, cost and quality objectives. When people are working collaboratively towards a common goal this is called ***teamwork*** and is a particularly cohesive and effective form of group working.

Teams are always made up of a group of people with varying technical and functional expertise. The effectiveness of the team will have a dramatic impact on the performance of the project. The most effective teams are not made up of people who have exactly the same outlook on life, the same preferences or the same habits. Bringing together a selection of people with different ideas and 'styles' is what will help the team to perform most effectively.

In the 1970s and 1980s it was very common for the entire project team to be co-located literally in one office. Today this is far less often the case, with the result that the virtual team, i.e. a team that doesn't usually meet face to face and is geographically dispersed, is becoming far more common. Managing a virtual team brings new challenges to project management, particularly when the team has never met face to face.

The challenge for the project manager is how to bring together a group of people and help them to bond and to work together as an effective and developing team focused on achieving the project success criteria and associated benefits. **Team building** and **team development** are difficult enough when the project

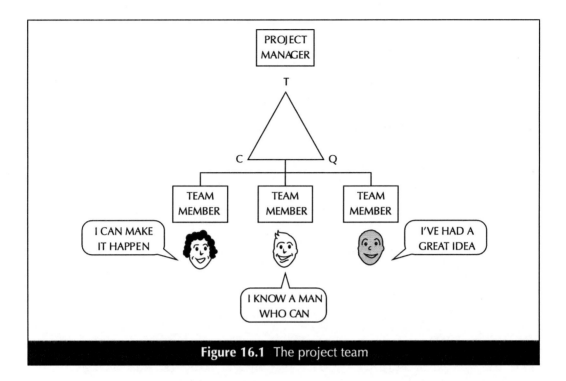

Figure 16.1 The project team

manager is able to choose his or her team, but in the majority of circumstances this is not possible and team members are 'allocated' to the project and the project manager works with what they have.

Project Red Nose Day

Although you have not been able to select all of your team members, you have been able to select the three event managers. In selecting them you have been proactive in making sure that you have chosen three different characters:

- event manager 1 is full of good ideas and always comes up with solutions to difficult problems
- event manager 2 is very good at ensuring that things get done, as well as being a good team-worker
- event manager 3 has a lot of good contacts with the company and is very reliable.

You are a stickler for detail and will be keen to monitor that things are going to plan.

You firmly believe that this mix of people you have put together will help you succeed in delivering the project, but you know that you will also need to take some actions to lead the team and help them work collaboratively towards the objectives.

Personal reflection

Think about the project teams that you have worked in.

What do you consider to be the factors that made the teams work well together (or not)?

Briefly describe your understanding of the characteristics of a typical project team and the things that can be done to improve team performance.

Think about real-life examples of top performing teams. What do you consider to be the factors that made those teams work well together?

_____

_____

_____

_____

_____

_____

_____

_____

_____

DEFINE LEADERSHIP AND THE ROLE OF THE LEADER

A group of people thrown together to form a project team is unlikely to work well together from the outset. They are likely to need some support with team building and development from someone in a leadership role. Within a project the project manager is expected to take the role of the **leader**.

Leadership is the ability to establish vision and direction, to influence and align others towards a common purpose, and to empower and inspire people to achieve project success. It enables the project to proceed in an environment of change and uncertainty.

For the team to start to perform in an effective manner it needs to be recognised that it will pass through a number of development stages. These stages are often known as forming (initial coming together), storming (disagreement on roles), norming (agreement on roles) and performing (carrying out the agreed roles). The names for the stages of team development outlined above were developed by Bruce Tuckmann, who found that teams develop in maturity and ability as relationships are established. He also noticed that effective team leaders change their style of management, beginning with a directing style, and moving through coaching, participating and delegating as the team develops.

Unfortunately some teams never make it to the performing stage and instead spend their time in forming and storming and, as a result, work very inefficiently and ineffectively. Project managers should take responsibility for helping the team to move quickly and effectively through the development stages, for example by communicating the vision and providing clear objectives, roles and responsibilities at the start, or by being willing to adopt a style that trusts the team members to decide how to perform activities as they become more mature. Because leaders need to be able to adopt different styles and approaches at different times, and they need to choose the most appropriate style and approach for a given situation, it is often said that the project manager should display situational leadership.

Figure 16.2 shows that for a group to perform as a team there needs to be a focus on objectives and also processes in place whereby individuals can learn and grow as a result of their experience. It is the leader's role to facilitate the transition from group to team. The leader of any project has a direct and significant impact on team performance.

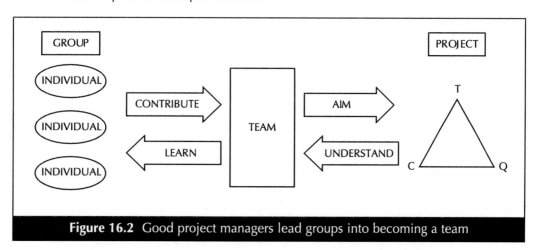

Figure 16.2 Good project managers lead groups into becoming a team

Project Red Nose Day

In order to overcome any initial team development problems you have arranged for a formal project launch meeting to take place immediately after the PMP has been agreed. The meeting will be attended by the:

- sponsor
- health and safety officer
- security adviser
- three event managers
- finance manager
- quality manager.

At this meeting you will confirm everyone's roles and responsibilities, as well as the project's objectives. After that you are hoping that the team will work well together and that there will be very little conflict, although you know that you will need to monitor this closely as any problems will affect your ability to deliver the project objectives. If conflicts do arise then you know that it will be your responsibility to intervene and try to find a resolution that protects relationships as well as the project objectives.

You have already spoken to each person involved while putting together the PMP, so you are hoping that there will be no surprises – but you can never be sure.

Personal reflection

Think about project teams that you have worked in.

Do you recognise the stages of team development from those experiences?

How successful was the project manager in leading the team towards achievement of objectives?

Briefly describe your views on what the leader needs to do to help move the team from a forming stage through to performing.

_____

_____

_____

_____

_____

_____

_____

_____

_____

Procurement 17

Topic 5.4 of the *APM Body of Knowledge* deals with procurement for projects and the need for a procurement strategy to guide decisions on what to buy, which suppliers to choose and the best ways to form contracts with suppliers. We carry out procurement all the time when we buy our groceries at the supermarket, purchase books or CDs on the internet or take a taxi ride. We may not do this very formally because we don't need to. Projects are different. For one thing we are usually spending someone else's money, perhaps lots of it, and things have to be delivered on time and to the right quality. The margin for error is usually less and the risks are usually higher, and therefore we need to think through actions more carefully.

DEFINE PROCUREMENT AND THE PURPOSE OF A PROCUREMENT STRATEGY

Procurement is defined as the securing of goods and services. There are other words that are often used synonymously with procurement including: purchasing, as in the purchasing of materials or equipment (goods), and contracting, as in the contracting of personnel or an organisation (services).

Not all projects will involve procurement. Many projects are delivered using in-house equipment, facilities and people. Other projects, such as the building of a new office block or the design and manufacture of new military equipment, will include a vast amount of procurement. The amount of procurement involved on these projects will often mean that the organisations involved will have their own procurement departments to manage this function on behalf of the project manager.

A key point to note, however, is that procurement is no different from other areas of project management in that the project manager is accountable for delivery of the project to the criteria approved in the project management plan (PMP). The procurement team and suppliers are part of the project team reporting to the project manager.

In projects where a lot of procurement needs to undertaken it is important to define a ***procurement strategy***. This will set out how goods and services will be acquired for the project. The procurement strategy will consider such factors as:

■ whether to make or buy what is needed, e.g. whether to design the software system from scratch or buy a ready-made system

- use of a single integrated supplier or multiple discrete suppliers, e.g. using one builder to do all the building works and be responsible for plumbing, electrical work and decorating, or using separate suppliers managed by you
- how suppliers will be selected, what form of contract will be used and how suppliers will be paid, e.g. will you have a competitive tender, will you contract under English law and will you pay against milestones or only upon completion?

RESOURCES	NEEDED	AVAILABLE	SHORTFALL
ANALYSTS	2	2	PROCURE
PROGRAMMERS	10	5	FROM
TRAINERS	2	1	SUPPLIERS
TESTERS	6	2	TO
PCs	10	10	SECURE
ROOM	1	1	RESOURCES

Figure 17.1 Project procurement process

It is the project manager's responsibility to ensure that certain key principles are followed when selecting and managing contractors and suppliers. These principles are designed to enable fair and amicable working arrangements between the two parties, i.e. the company or organisation and the contractor or supplier. Listed below are some of the key principles that a project manager should follow.

1 Use an objective process when selecting a contractor or supplier to avoid the influence of personal preferences (this would be part of the procurement strategy if one has been prepared)
2 Make sure there is understanding of what your organisation wants from the arrangement
3 Make sure there is understanding of what the contractor or supplier wants from the arrangement
4 Check out whether the contractor or supplier is really able to do the work that is required, to the required time, cost and quality objectives
5 Involve the contractor or supplier in project team activities wherever practicable to do so.

Project Red Nose Day

You only have £500 of the company's money to spend on the project unless you can persuade the sponsor to let you spend more or can find alternative sources of income. With such a small amount to spend, you are unlikely to want to place any contracts, but you are likely to purchase materials and services for promotion and communications. You are also considering purchasing T-shirts emblazoned with your company's logo and the Red Nose Day logo for all event organisers to wear.

Your procurement strategy for such a simple procurement activity doesn't have to consider many options. For obvious reasons you have no choice over whether to make or buy the T-shirts and it would be pointless going to more than one supplier. You would almost certainly ask a number of suppliers to give you a quote; you might even be able to do a good deal as the T-shirts are for a charitable event. Regarding payment it is likely that your supplier will require a large percentage or full payment with the order, so again there is little choice in this respect.

Personal reflection

Think about the projects that are conducted in your workplace.

Does the typical project include procurement of services and goods, or is most of the resource provided on an 'in-house' basis?

Have you seen the use of different procurement strategies when goods and services have been acquired from outside? If so, what have you seen?

Briefly describe your understanding of how you would manage procurement for a project in your organisation and how, as the project manager, you would retain control of the process.

_____

_____

_____

_____

_____

_____

_____

_____

_____

18 Project risk management

Topic 2.5 of the *APM Body of Knowledge* deals with project risk management and the purpose of the risk management process. The simplest definition of a project risk is an uncertainty that matters: it is about trying to anticipate the future and protect the project as far as possible from things that might happen. Formal risk management is considered by many experts in project management as the most beneficial technique on the basis that plans are 'educated guesses' and therefore all there is to manage is what might happen. If the project team just takes a chance that nothing bad will happen then it is likely that the project will require a degree of crisis management. Managing risks is intended to proactively avoid crises and to look for opportunities to do things even better.

DEFINE PROJECT RISK AND THE PURPOSE OF PROJECT RISK MANAGEMENT

A **project risk** is something that *might* occur: if it does, it *will* impact on one or more of the project's objectives, e.g. time, cost, quality or another of the project's success criteria. A key responsibility of the project manager is to prevent the consequences of such risk events negatively affecting the project and its stakeholders. Current thinking in project management is that risks can be both threats, i.e. things that can jeopardise the ability to meet objectives, or opportunities, i.e. things that can enhance the ability to meet objectives.

There is often confusion between project risks and project issues. Both risks and issues affect project objectives, but a risk is something that might happen and an issue is something that is happening – i.e. there is no uncertainty. Issues are covered in detail in Chapter 19.

Any project that is undertaken will contain risks because no one can reliably know what might happen in the future. Just as no one knows what numbers will win the Lotto next week or no one knows what horse will win the next Grand National, no one knows how a project will turn out. The purpose of **risk management** is to make projects less of a lottery so that specific objectives for change are more certain.

Typical project risks often relate to uncertainties around resource availability or uncertainties about the environment in which the project will take place. Examples of risks in these areas might be as follows:

- there may not be enough IT testing resource available to test the final system

- current employees may not have the skills required to work with the new technology
- we may get all the 'best' resources and things will be done more quickly
- planning permission may take longer to obtain than scheduled
- a change in government may mean a change in policy, making the project invalid
- it may be sunny every day, which would mean that the painting could be completed faster.

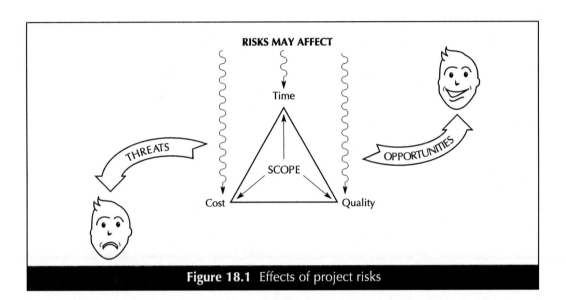

Figure 18.1 Effects of project risks

To manage risk, the project manager needs to carry out a structured process that enables individual risk events and overall project risk to be identified, understood and managed proactively, optimising project success by minimising threats and maximising opportunities.

Risks don't just exist for large or complex projects. All projects are susceptible to uncertainty and so risk management should be carried out regardless of project size. It is clear, though, that risk management isn't 'free' in a real sense. The effort put into managing the risk process costs the project money, and taking action to respond to identified risks will also cost money. The relationship between cost and benefit, however, is always seen as being a positive one.

The benefits of risk management that outweigh costs include the following:

- issues and problems cost more to solve than the costs of preventing them occurring
- plans are more accurate because estimates have taken account of risks
- stakeholders are more confident that plans are realistic and can be delivered.

Project Red Nose Day

There are a number of obvious risks associated with the *RND* project. Five of these are:

- you may be unable to secure enough volunteers to organise and run the actual events on the day
- an important company project may require that a key resource cannot meet its RND project obligations
- there may be more interest in the project than anticipated, resulting in an 'oversubscription' of the events planned
- someone may get hurt in one of the events
- someone may take offence at one of the events.

As project manager you need to deal with these risks, as they may well happen and if they do they will impact the project. The 'costs' of trying to manage the risks are very likely to be significantly less than the 'costs' of dealing with one or more issues if the risks are ignored.

Personal reflection

Think about a project you know well, either in the workplace or in a domestic or social setting.

What are the key risks that may jeopardise or enhance objectives?

Write a short list of risks that would affect objectives should they occur, remembering to use the word 'may' in the description, and remembering to think of 'upsides' or opportunities as well as 'downsides' or threats.

In your experience, is risk management seen as being 'worth it' for the project? If not, why might that be?

DEFINE A PROJECT RISK MANAGEMENT PROCESS

It is one thing to identify risks, but just identifying them does not do anything for the well-being of the project. Unlike the Lotto, where the outcome is truly uncertain, in most cases there are things that can be done to affect:

- whether a risk occurs or not, or if it occurs
- how much of an impact it might have on a project.

In order to do this, it is beneficial to carry out risk management in a consistent manner.

A typical **risk management process** would follow the steps listed below:

- initiate the risk management process
- identify risks (both threats and opportunities)
- assess the risks to see whether they are important or worth worrying about
- for those risks that are considered to be important, think of what could be done to respond to the risk in order to affect the chance that they will occur and the impact they would have on project objectives
- finally, make sure that the responses agreed above actually take place.

The risk management process doesn't only happen once on a project. It should be done during the project definition phase and then repeated throughout the life of the project.

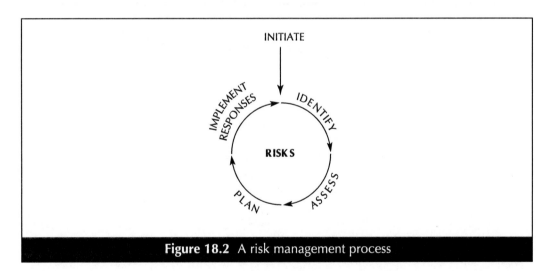

Figure 18.2 A risk management process

One key part of a project risk management process is the assignment of people to be *risk owners** for each risk that is identified. The project manager

---

Risk owner* – the person who has responsibility for dealing with a particular project risk and for identifying and managing responses.

always retains responsibility for the overall process, but he or she is not the person who is best placed to deal with every risk, nor to 'watch' the situation as the project progresses. Organisations who manage risks well understand the need for committed risk owners to be in place.

Project Red Nose Day

You have identified a number of risks to the RND project but nothing further has been done. Focusing on the risk that 'you may be unable to secure enough volunteers to organise and run the actual events on the day', you should probably consider this to be an important risk as it could seriously affect the amount you can raise and the whole spectacle of the day. You may want to reduce this risk by making sure that potential volunteers get plenty of notice. You may also try to think of incentives that might attract them to take part, such as personally meeting the visiting celebrity you have invited.

You need to find a risk owner for the risk. You decide you will take on this role yourself on this occasion but there are other risks that have been identified where you need someone else to be the risk owner.

The important thing to remember when it comes to risk management is that unless you actually do something – such as giving plenty of notice, or offering attractive incentives – you have not changed the risk at all, i.e. you haven't carried out risk management.

Personal reflection

Consider a project you know well that is now finished. List all the things that went wrong and the effect those things had on the project and project team.

Did the project use risk management to:

- identify risks
- allocate risk owners
- assess the importance of risks, by analysing their chance of occurring and their impact should they occur
- decide what actions to take to reduce the risk (either take away a threat or enhance an opportunity)
- monitor to make sure that planned actions were achieved?

Briefly describe how the risk management process used could have been improved to predict what might go wrong and to prevent those things having the impact they actually had.

_____

_____

_____

_____

_____

_____

_____

_____

DEFINE THE USE OF A RISK LOG (REGISTER)

All identified risks should be recorded in a risk log (some people call it a risk register – there is no difference). A **risk log** is a formal record of all identified risks, containing information such as:

- a description of the risk
- its chance of occurrence
- its likely impact
- who the risk owner is
- what action the risk owner intends to take.

The risk log also records either when the risk has occurred (and become an issue) or when it is no longer a risk for the project. It should be maintained through all phases of the project life cycle.

Id.	Description	Probability	Impact	Owner	Response/Action	Status
1	The company has no experience of the technology. We may not have the right expertise. This will lead to a delay in the project.	H	H	Design manager	Carry out an immediate audit of staff skills. If there is any shortfall, initiate a training and development programme.	Current
2	The company has never worked for this client. The client may change their requirements. This will lead to changes and increased profit for the company.	L	H	Project manager	Ensure that effective change control processes are in place and that the whole team is briefed on how they need to be used.	Current
3	The client is new to the UK. They may not understand their legal obligations. This will lead to a delay in getting project approvals.	M	M	Sponsor	Advise the client that we can help them to understand the legal system or suggest that they engage an appropriate law firm.	Closed

Figure 18.3 A simple risk log

As any action that is taken on the project can affect the ability to achieve time, cost and quality objectives and the wider success criteria, it is critical that risk owners work in partnership with the project manager. This is to ensure that decisions taken are in the best interest of the project as a whole. In particular, the risk log should highlight any constraints on risk owners: for example, the maximum costs they can expend dealing with a particular risk, or the time by which they have to achieve the desired response.

Project Red Nose Day

One of the risks you identified, 'there may be more interest in the project than anticipated', should ideally be owned by your boss as the sponsor. This risk is an opportunity in that the more people who are interested will mean the more money you raise. The risk owner (sponsor) needs to decide how to make this happen. Ignoring it will change nothing, whereas making some more company time available would enhance the chance significantly.

Personal reflection

Think of a project you know well, either at work or in a social context.

Think of an instance where the responsibility for managing a particular risk was delegated to someone else by the project manager.

Briefly describe how a risk log was used for the project and how the project manager kept control of the risk management process.

_____

_____

_____

_____

_____

_____

_____

_____

Issue management 19

Topic 3.8 of the *APM Body of Knowledge* deals with issue management. The word 'issue' is used in a very specific way in project management. During the life of the project problems will arise and the project manager has to deal with them. Some of these problems will be easily dealt with, while others will need support from the sponsor and other stakeholders before they can be resolved. Problems that fall into this category are called issues and are subject to issue management to remove the threats they pose.

DEFINE AN ISSUE, ISSUE MANAGEMENT AND THE USE OF AN ISSUE LOG (REGISTER)

Issues are problems or concerns that exist today and that will affect project objectives if not resolved, but where the project manager alone cannot resolve the situation. In such circumstances it is good practice for the project manager to capture issues in an ***issue log*** (sometimes called an issue register) so that they are not forgotten, a resolution is always obtained and there is a record of the things that happened and decisions taken to deal with them. This is ***issue management***.

Examples of issues might be:

- two of our key resources have left the company
- the prototype has failed all its initial tests
- Joe and Jane find it impossible to work together but are both essential project resources
- there are no suppliers that can meet our specification requirements
- prices received from bidders are at least twice more than we estimated.

You can see from this list of example issues that some of them regard people directly, such as Joe and Jane's difficulties in working together, while others are problems about deliverables, such as the prototype that failed initial tests. Although it is not always true that an unresolved issue will result in a conflict between people, it is often true. It follows then that one of the purposes of issue management is to prevent problems and concerns becoming crises for the project. Resolving conflicts between stakeholders and/or project team members requires special skills, takes time and costs money that could otherwise be put to better use.

Some people might say that resolving issues is just part of a manager's job, so why add bureaucracy by logging issues and monitoring them formally? There are three responses to this point. First, issues as described are not just any problem that needs resolution. Only if the concern or problem would cause a significant impact on the project if it wasn't resolved *and* the project manager cannot resolve it alone should an issue be raised.

The second point is that using an issue log means that issues are not forgotten and resource is allocated to see the issue through to a conclusion. In the same way that risks should be allocated a risk owner, then issues should be allocated an issue owner, the person best placed to resolve the issue on behalf of the project manager. The third point is that logging issues provides traceability of decisions made. This point is particularly important because there is a direct connection between issues, project changes and hence *change control**. Many issues that arise will not be able to be resolved without changing one of the project's objectives or the scope, and as a result there will almost certainly be some effect on the business case. Project changes that arise as the result of an issue, like all other changes, need to be the subject of change control. This is the subject of Chapter 20.

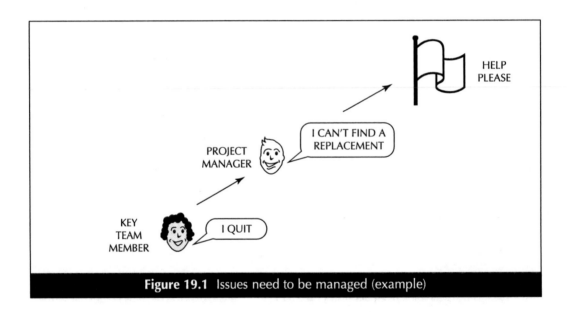

Figure 19.1 Issues need to be managed (example)

---

* Change control – a process that ensures that all changes made to a project's baseline scope, cost, time or quality objectives are identified, evaluated, approved, rejected or deferred.

Project Red Nose Day

It is traditional in your company that on one Friday every year a large proportion of staff take time off to play in an interdepartment golf match. You have just been made aware that the date being discussed for this is the same day as RND is planned for. Obviously RND cannot change, and so you have an issue which needs resolving. There is no way that you, as the project manager, can instruct the golf match organisers to change their date. As both your boss and the managing director are invited to participate in the golf match you feel that escalating the issue to them will provide your best chance of achieving a resolution.

Personal reflection

Think about a project you know well.

Consider the definition of issue provided.

Briefly describe how you have seen issues being dealt with in your experience. Were issues progressed in a formal manner with an issue log?

What do you believe to be the pros and cons of a formal approach to issue management from your experience?

_____

_____

_____

_____

_____

_____

_____

_____

_____

20 Change control

Topic 3.5 in the *APM Body of Knowledge* deals with change control, which is the process that the project manager implements to make sure that the business case and PMP remain up to date through the phases of the project life cycle. The process starts from the point where a change is requested, often verbally. It progresses through a decision-making stage about whether to implement the change or not, and concludes with communication and documentation of the results of the decision. Change control can seem an overly bureaucratic process at first glance, but those who have experienced the impact of unmanaged project changes have come to appreciate the process the hard way.

DEFINE PROJECT CHANGE AND THE USE OF A CHANGE REQUEST

A project is the means by which new products, services or improvements are developed and introduced in a controlled way. All projects should start off with defined time, cost, quality objectives and other success criteria, linked to the scope of work that will achieve them. In an ideal world, these parameters would remain constant. We don't live in an ideal world and, as a result, it is very unlikely that the objectives and scope of the project will remain constant throughout the project life cycle. ***Project changes*** will occur, and when they do it will probably be for one of the following reasons:

- a change in justification for the project
- a change in requirements to the scope or specification of deliverables
- the discovery of a mistake or error
- an incorrect estimate
- a reduction in resource availability
- a technological or market place change.

The result of any of the above will trigger a ***change request***. A change request may arise through changes in the business or issues affecting the project. Because such requests will inevitably change the plans for the project, and often the business case, they must be taken seriously and evaluated systematically.

It is important to note the use of the word request. A change request is just that – it is not an order to change (although some stakeholders will be more influential than others and will need a very good justification if the request is to be rejected). The request is the trigger for a change to be formally considered.

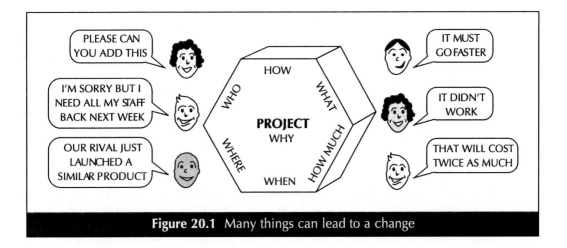

Figure 20.1 Many things can lead to a change

Project Red Nose Day

The company's managing director has just bumped into you in the corridor and asked you what would be the effect on the RND project if you were to arrange six events on the day rather than three. He was very keen to point out that this was not an instruction, but this does amount to being a change request.

Personal reflection

Think about a project you know well.
  Consider the list of potential triggers for change requests:

- a change in justification for the project
- a change in requirements to the scope or specification of deliverables
- the discovery of a mistake or error
- an incorrect estimate
- a reduction in resource availability.

Briefly write down a specific example of each one of the potential triggers that may affect a project you know.

_____

_____

_____

_____

_____

_____

_____

DEFINE PROJECT CHANGE CONTROL

One of the key responsibilities of a project manager during the implementation phase of the project is the application and administration of formal change control.

Project change control is a means by which project change requests are recorded, evaluated, authorised and managed. Without this process, there would be a 'free for all', with perhaps those who shout the loudest being the ones to get what they want. This is not the best scenario for the project as a whole. Without formal change control the project's scope is likely to creep (gradually increase) and, as a result, the cost will increase and probably the end date will slip. A project that costs more than originally anticipated and that takes longer may well not achieve its success criteria and therefore fail to meet its business case.

If you are a project manager it is inevitable that you will get informal requests to make changes on a project, e.g. you might be asked to purchase some new desktop PCs as part of the roll-out of the new IT system. Even though you might think that it is the right thing to do to buy the new PCs, and there is enough money in the budget to do so, this request, like all other change requests, should be subjected to formal change control. Only if this is done might you become aware that there is another project in progress that will replace all desktop PCs with laptops.

Formal change control is the method that ensures that the project plans are kept up to date throughout the project life cycle.

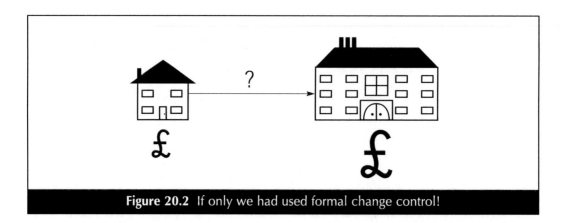

Figure 20.2 If only we had used formal change control!

Project Red Nose Day

Your managing director could have adopted a more forceful approach when requesting the change. He could have said that you were to ignore any change control process and 'just do it'. If you had chosen to take this approach there is a good chance that when the project was over it would become apparent that the 1000 hours maximum of staff time specified as a constraint had been exceeded. It is also quite likely that your boss (the sponsor) would not be too pleased about this, so the 'just do it' approach must be avoided even if the change process used to agree changed plans is relatively informal.

Personal reflection

Think of a project situation that you know well.

Implementing formal change control takes discipline, but it is necessary to prevent scope creep and subsequent loss of control of the time, cost and quality objectives of the project.

Briefly describe the problems that need to be overcome when implementing a formal system to manage change requests.

_____

_____

_____

_____

_____

_____

_____

_____

_____

DEFINE THE ACTIVITIES INVOLVED IN A CHANGE CONTROL PROCESS AND THE USE OF THE CHANGE LOG (REGISTER)

A formal **change control process** should be applied to all projects. Formal change control encompasses four main stages: recording of the proposed change, evaluation or impact assessment, authorisation (or not) and management.

Proposed project changes are usually documented on a change request form and then recorded or logged in a **change log** (change register means exactly the same thing). All changes need to be recorded in the change log. The change log lists all project changes whatever their status: proposed, authorised, rejected or deferred. A change log is usually depicted as a table created in word-processing software, or a spreadsheet or database that lists key aspects of a change. These will include:

- a unique number for the change
- who requested it
- a description of the change request
- impact assessment:
  - time
  - cost
  - quality
  - other success criteria
  - stakeholder expectations
  - risks

- cumulative effect on objectives
- status of the change
- date when a decision was made.

Most project managers find keeping the change log up to date an invaluable aid both during the project and at the end of it. During the project it will help in understanding the changes that are in the pipeline and their potential impact on the project. At the end of the project it will allow the project manager to explain, if explanation is needed, why the project cost more or less than planned, took a longer or shorter time than planned or why the quality of the deliverables varied from the plan.

As you can see from the list of fields in the change log, once logged, the change is then subjected to a review which will include an impact assessment. The results of this impact assessment are included on both the change request form and in the change log. The assessed change should then be submitted to the appropriate authority who will do one of three things: authorise the change, reject it or defer it. Typical authorities might be the sponsor or a change control board, or in some cases the project manager may authorise changes to a certain limit.

Whichever response is made, the person who requested the change should be informed of the decision. Changes that are authorised must then be managed, and this will include updating the overall project management plan (PMP) and any associated and detailed documentation, such as the project schedule and the budget.

For example, as the project manager for a new computer system, you may receive a change request from one of the key users for more functionality. Even though they might have a very compelling argument why this change needs to be implemented, you must still apply change control. After logging the change, all the consequences of its impact must be assessed, including doing nothing. If, after assessment of the change, the decision is to reject it, then it is your responsibility to communicate this to the user who requested the change. If the decision is to accept it, then you must rework all the project plans accordingly.

Project Red Nose Day

You have just found out that the reason why the managing director has requested a change is because there is an issue. It needs resolving and a project change might be one of the ways to do it. The issue is that a number of staff are feeling left out of the fun. They feel that only three events will prevent them from actively participating. As a result, some staff are becoming quite anti the whole thing. This is the last thing you or the company want. You cannot resolve this issue yourself, but it looks as though your MD may have pre-empted the problem and is trying to assist in its resolution by requesting a change.

The process you are informally adopting is a good example of a change control process. You have received notification of a change request which you would be wise to confirm in writing, perhaps via email. Assuming you are running a change log, you will have registered the change request in it. The impact assessment you have carried out should be documented, along

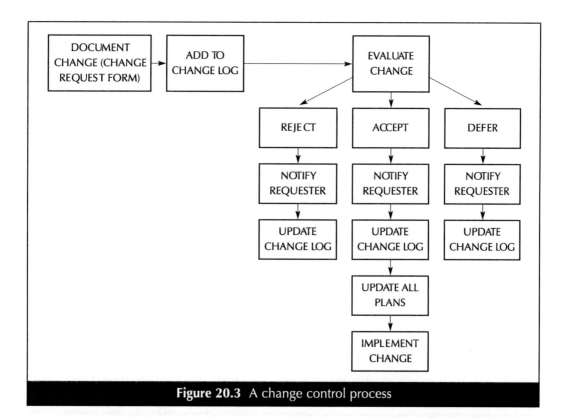

Figure 20.3 A change control process

with the reason for the change, and submitted to the sponsor for approval or rejection (deferral is not an option here).

If the sponsor approves the change, then you must update the project objectives and plans accordingly and notify all those involved of the changes. If the sponsor rejects the change, then you must inform the requester (the managing director) that this is the case and find another way of handling the project issue about the involvement of staff and their commitment to the project.

Personal reflection

Think of a project that you know well.

How was project change controlled?

Briefly describe the stages of the process and your views on how effective this process proved to be.

_____

_____

_____

_____

_____

_____

_____

_____

_____

Configuration 21
management

Topic 4.7 in the *APM Body of Knowledge* deals with configuration management, which some would say is just a more complex way of saying version control. The official APM definition of the term *configuration** seems grand and could be confusing but the practicalities are much simpler. Managing the configuration actually means making sure that all the pieces of the project 'jigsaw' can be identified, that they fit together and that they are documented in a way that replacement pieces could be made if it became necessary. In some ways configuration management is closely related to specifications as part of project quality management (Chapter 12). In other ways it is closely related to change control (Chapter 20) because any approved change will affect the configuration. Getting configuration management right is a critical success factor for projects, which is why the subject warrants a separate topic in the *APM Body of Knowledge.*

DEFINE CONFIGURATION MANAGEMENT IN TERMS OF CONFIGURATION IDENTIFICATION AND CONTROL

Configuration is the word used to describe the sum of the different elements of the project that need to be controlled. Some of these elements might be physical things such as a component of a bridge, some elements might be software code and others will be documents or drawings. Each different element is called a configuration item and must be identified through **configuration identification**. Configuration items must have a unique identification and a specific purpose, and they must all be controlled through configuration management.

Configuration management is the administrative work that needs to be done to create unique identities for configuration items and to control changes as they occur. Configuration management is the responsibility of the project manager.

While some relate to configuration management as version control, others say that configuration management is best described as very detailed change control.

---

* Configuration – functional and physical characteristics of a product as defined in technical documents and achieved in the product. Note: in a project this should contain all items that can be identified as being relevant to the project and that should only be modified after authorisation by the relevant manager.

Change control and configuration management are necessarily linked because an authorised project change always results in at least one configuration item needing to be updated.

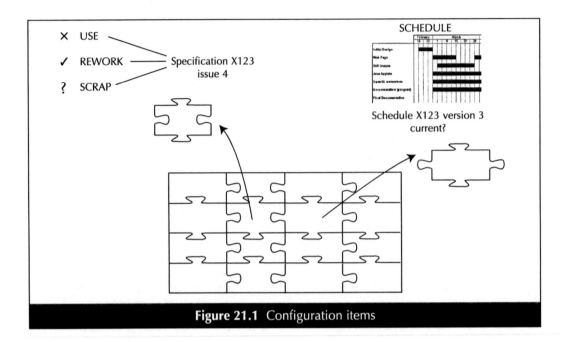

Figure 21.1 Configuration items

For example, in a project to install new signage across a company, a configuration item would be the company's logo and another would be the font to be used. If anything changed on the logo or the font during the life of the project this would obviously have a significant impact on all the signage.

Another example is the control of drawings in any design project. Each drawing is itself a configuration item. Any change in any drawing will need to be reflected in any other affected drawings and also in other areas such as sizes of materials or equipment. In this example, as in many others, configuration management tends to be seen as document or version control.

If a problem during project implementation arises, the project manager will need to refer to the previous specifications of each configuration item. Traceability, for accounting purposes, and accountability, for communication with stakeholders, are both key parts of configuration management and are achieved with the help of accurate and up-to-date documentation. This must be securely held and kept up to date.

If the example of design drawings is considered again, then suitable documentation in this case would be a register of some description that recorded the following:

- the title of the drawing, with a unique identification code or number (the configuration item)
- a revision or version number
- its current approval status.

This kind of documentation needs to be in place for each configuration item. It is also essential that, from a 'top-down' perspective, there is a clear picture of how each individual configuration item affects other items. For example, if a logo is a configuration item, which other items would need to be changed if the logo had to change?

In many organisations, this overall record of the project configuration, a document which shows the status of each configuration item, is best maintained by a person who has the role of configuration librarian. That person often works within a project support office. Other organisations may manage this function through the quality department. Where such support is not in place, the project manager must do the work him- or herself.

UNIQUE IDENTIFIER	VERSION	STATUS	USED ON
AAA	1	SUPERSEDED	ABC, AFQ
AAA	2	CURRENT	ABC, AFQ
AAB	1	CURRENT	BAD, CAB
AAC	1	CURRENT	ZYW, XFG
etc.			

Figure 21.2 Configuration item status

The fundamental point is that configuration management is a way of maintaining control of the constituent parts of the project. Changes at all levels must be subjected to **configuration control** so that each configuration item's status can be controlled and logged. This means that, at any point in time, all the project team can recognise the current version of any item. Working, in any way, on superseded items must be avoided.

Project Red Nose Day

One of the configuration items that you have identified for the project is the name of the celebrity who will pay a visit to your company on the day of the event. The celebrity's name will be used on all communication media and is a key part of your risk management process.

Remember that you promised to introduce all participants to her, and you need to plan accordingly. As you can see, if the celebrity is changed, it would have a considerable knock-on effect throughout the rest of the project.

Another configuration item is the Red Nose Day and Comic Relief charity logo. You may be pretty certain that it isn't going to change in the next ten weeks, but it would make sense to confirm this.

Personal reflection

Reflect on your experience of working in projects, either in the workplace or in a domestic or social situation.

Can you recognise the concept of the configuration items and see how the status of the configuration items was controlled?

Briefly describe a number of configuration items from your experience and the processes used to make sure that everyone worked with the most up-to-date version.

_____

_____

_____

_____

_____

_____

_____

_____

_____

Information management 22

Topic 3.7 in the *APM Body of Knowledge* deals with information management, the collection, storage, distribution, archiving and (eventual) appropriate destruction of project information. Included in this topic is project reporting which is dealt with in detail below. Other aspects of information management are not included in this book although the project manager is responsible for making sure adequate arrangements are in place.

DEFINE PROJECT REPORTING

One of the main duties of a project manager is to report on the status of the project; this is known as **project reporting**. In essence, project reporting takes information about the project and presents it in an appropriate format to stakeholders and in line with the project communication plan. It is implied by the term 'reporting' that most reports are written (or in reality printed from computer software); however, reports can equally be verbal via progress meetings or conference calls.

Reporting tends to be a formal process with reports issued or presented either:

- in line with an agreed calendar, e.g. monthly
- at predetermined points in the life cycle, e.g. at the end of every phase, or
- after a significant activity has taken place.

The project manager will produce reports that cover topics such as progress against the schedule, expenditure against the budget and performance against the quality plan, the latest predicted end date and also against agreed key performance indicators (KPIs). There will also be reports produced as a result of audits, project reviews and risk assessments.

Reporting these things will give an indication of whether or not the project will deliver the required benefit, and if there is underperformance then remedial action can be taken before it is too late.

When reporting on projects it is often useful to consider a technique known as reporting by exception. This means that if everything is going to plan then almost nothing is said or written. Only when things are not going to plan, i.e. things are ahead of or behind schedule, there is underspending or overspending, or quality is better or worse than planned, is a report made. Although reporting by exception is a means to reduce the burden of reporting, it requires a level of trust between the project manager and stakeholders that no news is good news and anything to the contrary will be reported and not ignored.

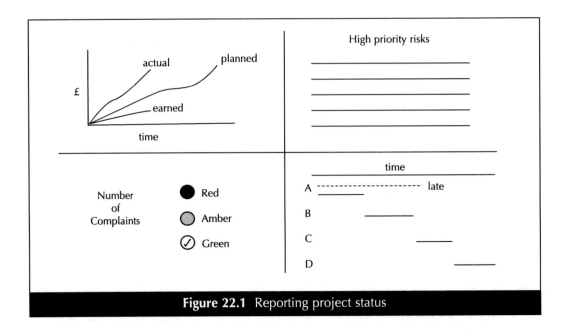

Figure 22.1 Reporting project status

Project Red Nose Day

In the communication plan you agreed with your boss (the sponsor) that you would meet on a formal one-to-one basis each week throughout the project. Your boss is aware of the principles of exception reporting and wants you to update her at each weekly meeting only on the things that are not going to plan.

You also have a weekly progress meeting with the project team. At this meeting you will present progress against the schedule, and expenditure against the budget. In addition you will also report how many hours have been booked against the project, remembering you only have 1000 hours to play with.

You will use the company's notice boards to report how much sponsorship money has been pledged to date. You intend to update this on a daily basis if the data can be made available.

Personal reflection

Think about projects you know well and the typical reporting methods that you have seen.

Are the reports effective?

How might the reports be improved?

Is exception reporting being used in any way?

Briefly describe how you think project reporting could be improved from your experience.

_____

_____

_____

_____

_____

_____

_____

_____

_____

23 Handover and closeout

Topic 6.5 in the *APM Body of Knowledge* deals with handover and closeout, the generic name given to the final phase in the project life cycle. During this phase the project deliverables are handed over to the sponsor and users, who are hopefully delighted with the results. Closeout is the process of finishing the project and broadly covers two areas. First, administration, which could be seen as the boring part after all the excitement of the project, and second, learning for the future, which is hopefully seen as important and worthwhile.

DEFINE THE ACTIVITIES INVOLVED IN HANDOVER AND CLOSEOUT

Projects are used to deliver specific objectives for change. Just as projects need a controlled start and a controlled middle, they also need a controlled end.

At the completion of any project the project manager must ensure that the products or deliverables are handed over to whoever is going to use them. In order to do this it is beneficial for the project manager to follow an agreed handover and closeout process.

Prior to **handover** the project manager must make sure that the project's deliverables or products meet the defined acceptance criteria. This may include formal testing or application of other quality controls. As a result of these tests or checks, the chance that the deliverables will be considered unacceptable by the end user will be minimised. Most project managers will require that the end user, either an external customer or the organisation's operational business, signs a certificate of acceptance to confirm that the deliverables have been handed over and are acceptable. This is important particularly to mark the official 'transfer of ownership' of deliverables, which can be critical for contractual purposes for some projects.

During **closeout** the project manager must make sure that all project finance and general administration are completed. This will avoid the carry-over of work and will formally signify the completion of the project. The project manager is also responsible for disbanding the project team and making sure that each team member, including contractors, has finalised their work. The project manager must also conduct a post-project review (described in Chapter 24).

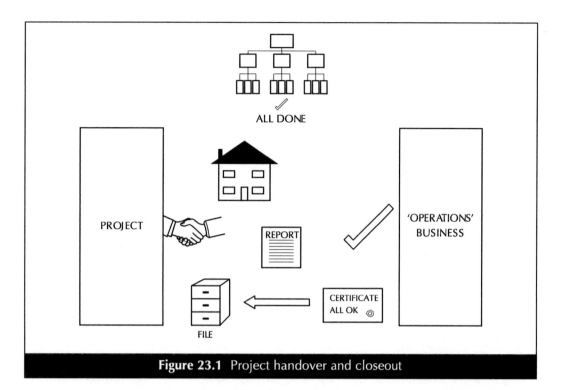

Figure 23.1 Project handover and closeout

Project Red Nose Day

Handover of the RND project will occur just prior to the presentation of the cheque to the Comic Relief charity. When this point is reached it is important that the following checks have been made:

■ all donations have been collected
■ there are no outstanding bills or invoices to be paid
■ all work is completed and no more company time will be used.

Handover will take place from the project manager to sponsor. It will be the sponsor who makes the presentation to Comic Relief.

Personal reflection

Consider the projects you know well.

How is handover from the temporary project organisation to the operational business carried out? Is this a controlled process?

Briefly describe your understanding of the importance of this stage in the process and your thoughts on the critical aspects of handover from your experience.

Project reviews 24

Topic 6.6 in the *APM Body of Knowledge* deals with the project reviews that take place throughout the project life cycle to check progress against plans. There are a number of different terms used for project reviews, including project evaluation reviews, project audits, gate reviews, post-project reviews and benefits realisation reviews; the latter may take place some time after handover and closeout. Whatever the terms used, project reviews are always about making sure that the project manager, sponsor and other stakeholders know how things are going. In this chapter we will look specifically at two types of review, the gate review and the post-project review, but will refer to the others to try to make sense of all the different terms used.

DEFINE GATE REVIEWS

The idea of the **gate review** is closely linked to the phases of the project life cycle. As already explained in Chapter 4, one of the primary reasons for dividing any project into phases is to assist with decision-making at key points. It is now common practice to refer to the end of a phase within the project life cycle as a 'gate' or 'gateway'. Each gate is a decision point where senior stakeholders can decide whether to continue with the next phase as planned, or to change plans or cancel the project. The gate review is the process that the decision-makers go through at each gate. Each gate review should be informed by progress to date, future plans and a review of the current circumstances. Results from project audits or from project evaluation reviews during the phase in question may inform a gate review.

Organisations that do this process well are confident that they work only on projects that are going to deliver the desired success criteria and benefits. This is useful not only to senior managers who are making the investment decisions but also to the project manager and project team as they know they are always doing work that is valued. Effective gate reviews stop projects that no longer meet the organisation's needs.

Project Red Nose Day

As described in Chapter 4 and Figure 4.2, the RND project will have gate reviews at the end of each phase. A short meeting was held with the sponsor once the event design and the PMP were complete, and as a result of this some modifications were made to plans in order to meet the project success criteria for media coverage. It was useful to have this sanity check before pressing ahead with the communication phase of the project.

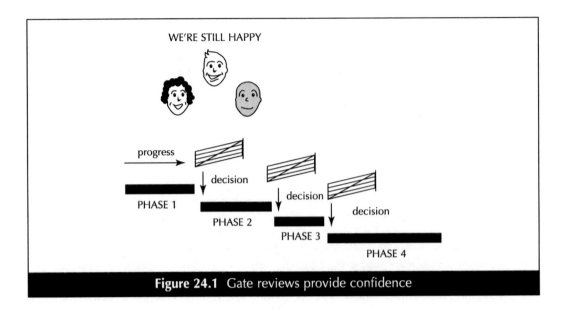

Figure 24.1 Gate reviews provide confidence

Personal reflection

Think about a project you know well.

Were gate reviews carried out as a way of confirming that the project was progressing down the right track?

To your knowledge has a project ever been stopped at a gate review?

Briefly describe your thoughts about what is needed to make gate reviews work well as 'go/no-go' decision points for a project.

_____

_____

_____

_____

_____

_____

_____

_____

DEFINE POST-PROJECT REVIEWS

All projects should undertake a **post-project review** to ensure that the experience of the project is recorded for the benefit of others, i.e. to learn lessons. This documented review of the project's performance is produced after the handover of deliverables is complete and during project closeout but before the project is actually closed. It is another responsibility of the project manager.

In carrying out the review the project manager will seek to compare the final outcome of the project with the currently approved project success criteria, which should be contained in both the business case and PMP. If these criteria have all been met the project should be considered a success. The project should not be closed until all project success criteria can be confirmed; however, this does not mean that all the benefits from the project will have been realised at closeout. In such cases a benefits realisation review should be planned at some later date, but this is the responsibility of the sponsor, not the project manager.

To complete the post-project review the project manager and other key members of the project team will also need to look at other project documentation, such as:

- the business case
- the project management plan (PMP)
- the risk log
- the change log
- the issue log
- project reports.

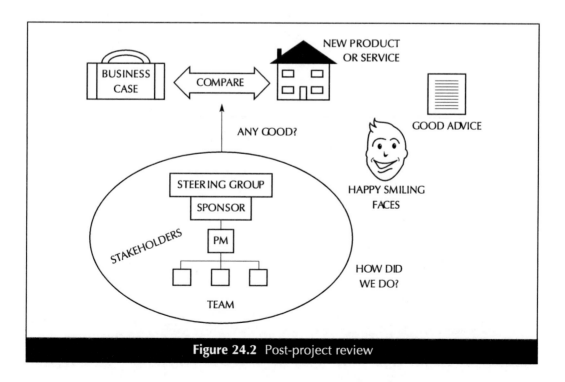

Figure 24.2 Post-project review

Post-project reviews allow the organisation to continuously improve by learning from experience. Some people would say that learning from experience prevents 'the same mistake being made twice' or 'reinventing the wheel at every opportunity', but the lessons to be learned from projects need not always be seen as negative. On most projects there are things that go right just as there are things that go wrong. It is important to understand both of these facets. It is even more important to understand what caused the things to go right and wrong, as the effect they had on the project will probably be quite obvious. Understanding the cause of something that went right will allow it to be done again; likewise, understanding the cause of something that went wrong may allow it to be avoided next time.

The following are examples of things that can be improved as a result of learning from experience:

- selection of suppliers
- identification of risks
- estimating accuracy for project and activity durations and costs
- resource deployment.

Project Red Nose Day

As project manager, you have the responsibility of undertaking a post-project review. In order for the review to be effective you should ensure that the following people attend:

- the sponsor
- the health and safety officer
- the security adviser
- the three event managers
- the finance manager
- the quality manager
- three 'representative event participants'.

As part of the review you will consider all the project documentation that has been prepared. One aim of the review will be for you to determine whether the project was a success or not by comparing the final outcome with the agreed project success criteria.

The other aim of the review will be for you to suggest how things could be improved if the company had a Red Nose Day or some other fundraising event at some time in the future.

A potential example of a lesson to be learned could relate to the design of the sponsorship forms. You are considering delaying the start of this activity by one week. If you do this it might mean that less money will be raised because of the shorter time between distributing the forms and Red Nose Day. Should this risk occur, the underlying cause of the effect would have been that you wrongly re-prioritised this work, rather than seeking assistance to make sure it happened as originally planned.

Personal reflection

Think about projects you are familiar with that are handed over and closed.
  Was a post-project review conducted?
  Were lessons learned made available to the wider organisation?
  Briefly describe your experience of post-project review and your thoughts
about the importance of this step for every project.

_____

_____

_____

_____

_____

_____

_____

_____

_____

Appendices

Appendix 1: Introductory Certificate syllabus

All of the syllabus elements should be taken within the context of a project and project management.
The reading list for the Introductory Certificate contains only two books: *APM Body of Knowledge 5th edition* and *Starting Out in Project Management. 2nd edition*

BoK topic	Title	Topic coverage	Learning outcomes
1	**Project Management in Context**		
1.1	Project Management	■ Definitions – project, project management ■ Projects versus business-as-usual ■ Project management processes ■ Time – cost – quality/performance ■ Purpose of project management	A. Define a project B. Define project management C. Define the differences between a project and business-as-usual D. Define project management processes E. Define the relationship between time, cost and quality/performance
1.2	Programme Management	■ Definitions – programme, programme management	A. Define a programme B. Define programme management

BoK topic	Title	Topic coverage	Learning outcomes
1.3	Portfolio Management	■ Definitions – portfolio, portfolio management	A. Define a portfolio B. Define portfolio management
1.4	Project Context	■ The context and environment of a project ■ PESTLE as a tool	A. Define project context
1.5	Project Sponsorship	■ Definitions – project sponsor (executive), project sponsorship	A. Define project sponsorship
1.6	Project Office	*Not included in the IC syllabus*	
2	**Planning the Strategy**		
2.1	Project Success and Benefits Management	■ Definitions – project success criteria, key performance indicators (KPIs), success factors, benefit ■ Purpose of benefits management	A. Define project success criteria B. Define key performance indicators (KPIs) C. Define success factors D. Define benefit
2.2	Stakeholder Management	■ Definitions – stakeholders, stakeholder management ■ Stakeholder analysis as a tool	A. Define stakeholder B. Define stakeholder management C. Define stakeholder analysis
2.3	Value Management	*Not included in the IC syllabus*	
2.4	Project Management Plan	■ Contents and purpose of the project management plan (PMP) ■ Authorship, approval and audience for the PMP	A. Define project management plan (PMP) B. Define the purpose of a PMP C. Define the benefits of a PMP D. Define the contents of a PMP E. Define the ownership of a PMP

BoK topic	Title	Topic coverage	Learning outcomes
2.5	Project Risk Management	■ Definitions – risk, risk management ■ Risk management process ■ Risk owner ■ Use of a risk log (register) ■ Purpose of risk management	A. Define project risk B. Define project risk management C. Define a project risk management process D. Define the use of a risk log (register)
2.6	Project Quality Management	■ Definitions – quality, quality management ■ Quality planning, quality assurance and quality control ■ Purpose of quality management	A. Define quality B. Define quality management C. Define the differences between quality planning, quality assurance and quality control
2.7	Health, Safety and Environmental Management	*Not included in the IC syllabus*	
3	**Executing the Strategy**		
3.1	Scope Management	■ Definitions – project scope, scope management ■ Product breakdown structure (PBS), work breakdown structure (WBS), cost breakdown structure (CBS), organisational breakdown structure (OBS) ■ Responsibility assignment matrix (RAM)	A. Define project scope B. Define project scope management C. Define the uses of a product breakdown structure (PBS) D. Define the uses of a work breakdown structure (WBS) E. Define the uses of a cost breakdown structure (CBS) F. Define the uses of an organisational breakdown structure (OBS)

BoK topic	Title	Topic coverage	Learning outcomes
3.1 cont'd			G. Define the purpose of a responsibility assignment matrix (RAM) H. Define the uses of a responsibility assignment matrix (RAM)
3.2	Scheduling	■ Definitions – scheduling, activities, network diagrams, Gantt (bar) charts, critical path, total float, milestones, baseline ■ Purpose of scheduling	A. Define scheduling B. Define total float C. Define the term critical path D. Define Gantt (bar) chart E. Define baseline F. Define milestone
3.3	Resource Management	■ Definitions – types of resources, resource management, resource allocation, resource smoothing (time-limited scheduling) and resource levelling (resource-limited scheduling) ■ Purpose of resource management	A. Define resource management B. Define resource smoothing (time-limited scheduling) C. Define resource levelling (resource-limited scheduling)
3.4	Budgeting and Cost Management	*Not included in the IC syllabus*	
3.5	Change Control	■ Definitions – change, change control ■ Change control activities ■ Change requests ■ Use of a change log (register) ■ Purpose of change control ■ Links to configuration management	A. Define project change B. Define project change control C. Define the activities involved in project change control D. Define the use of a change request E. Define the use of a change log (register)

BoK topic	Title	Topic coverage	Learning outcomes
3.6	Earned Value Management	*Not included in the IC syllabus*	
3.7	Information Management and Reporting	■ Definition of project reporting ■ Project reports (progress, quality, audit, project reviews, risk assessment and finances)	A. Define project reporting
3.8	Issue Management	■ Definitions – issue, issue management ■ Use of an issue log (register) ■ Ownership	A. Define an issue B. Define issue management C. Define the use of an issue log (register)
4	**Techniques**		
4.1	Requirements Management	*Not included in the IC syllabus*	
4.2	Development	*Not included in the IC syllabus*	
4.3	Estimating	■ Definitions – estimates ■ Primary estimating methods (bottom-up, comparative, parametric) ■ The concept of the estimating funnel	A. Define what an estimate is B. Define bottom-up estimating C. Define comparative estimating D. Define parametric estimating
4.4	Technology Management	*Not included in the IC syllabus*	
4.5	Value Engineering	*Not included in the IC syllabus*	
4.6	Modelling and Testing	*Not included in the IC syllabus*	

BoK topic	Title	Topic coverage	Learning outcomes
4.7	Configuration Management	■ Definitions – configuration management ■ Activities in configuration management ■ Importance of configuration management ■ Links to change control	A. Define configuration management
5	**Business and Commercial**		
5.1	Business Case	■ Definitions – business case ■ Content and purpose of a business case ■ Ownership and audience of a business case	A. Define the purpose of a business case B. Define the ownership of a business case
5.2	Marketing and Sales	*Not included in the IC syllabus*	
5.3	Project Financing and Funding	*Not included in the IC syllabus*	
5.4	Procurement	■ Definitions – procurement ■ The purpose of a procurement strategy	A. Define procurement
5.5	Legal Awareness	*Not included in the IC syllabus*	
6	**Organisation and Governance**		
6.1	Project Life Cycles	■ Definitions – project life cycle ■ Phases (concept, definition, implementation, handover and closeout) ■ Reasons for splitting projects into phases	A. Define a project life cycle B. Define the phases for a project life cycle C. Define the reasons for splitting projects into phases

BoK topic	Title	Topic coverage	Learning outcomes
6.2	Concept	*Not included in the IC syllabus*	
6.3	Definition	*Not included in the IC syllabus*	
6.4	Implementation	*Not included in the IC syllabus*	
6.5	Handover and Closeout	■ Definitions – handover, closeout ■ Activities of handover and closeout ■ Importance of handover and closeout	A. Define handover B. Define closeout C. Define the activities involved in handover and closeout
6.6	Project Reviews	■ Definitions – project evaluation reviews, gate reviews, audits, post-project reviews, benefit realisation reviews ■ Importance of project reviews	A. Define gate reviews B. Define post-project reviews
6.7	Organisation Structure	*Not included in the IC syllabus*	
6.8	Organisational Roles	■ Definitions – project manager, project sponsor (executive), users, project team members and the project steering group (project board) ■ Responsibilities of project manager, project sponsor (executive), users, project team members and the project steering group (project board)	A. Define the responsibilities of the project manager B. Define the responsibilities of the project sponsor (executive) C. Define the responsibilities of the users D. Define the responsibilities of the project team members E. Define the responsibilities of the project steering group (project board)

BoK topic	Title	Topic coverage	Learning outcomes
6.9	Methods and Procedures	*Not included in the IC syllabus*	
6.10	Governance of Project Management	*Not included in the IC syllabus*	
7	**People and the Profession**		
7.1	Communication	■ Definition – communication ■ Methods of communication ■ Media used in communication ■ Importance and contents of a communication plan	A. Define communication B. Define the contents of a communication plan
7.2	Teamwork	■ Definitions – project team, teamwork, team development models	A. Define project team B. Define teamwork
7.3	Leadership	■ Definitions – leadership ■ Impact on team performance ■ Role of a leader	A. Define leadership B. Define the role of a leader
7.4	Conflict Management	*Not included in the IC syllabus*	
7.5	Negotiation	*Not included in the IC syllabus*	
7.6	Human Resource Management	*Not included in the IC syllabus*	
7.7	Behavioural Characteristics	*Not included in the IC syllabus*	
7.8	Learning and Development	*Not included in the IC syllabus*	
7.9	Professionalism and Ethics	*Not included in the IC syllabus*	

Appendix 2: Chapters in *Starting Out in Project Management* mapped against the APM Introductory Certificate in Project Management syllabus

Starting Out in Project Management chapter	APM Introductory Certificate in Project Management syllabus topic(s)
1	1.1
2	1.2 & 1.3
3	1.5 & 6.8
4	6.1
5	1.4
6	2.2
7	2.1
8	7.1
9	5.1
10	2.4
11	3.1
12	2.6
13	4.3
14	3.2
15	3.2
16	7.2 & 7.3
17	5.4
18	2.5
19	3.8
20	3.5
21	4.7
22	3.7
23	6.5
24	6.6

Appendix 3: Comparison between fourth and fifth editions of the *APM Body of Knowledge*

Fourth edition, 2000[a]	Fifth edition, 2006[b]	Comments
1 General	*1 Project management in context*	All topics renumbered. Section name changed
10 Project Management	**1.1 Project management**	
11 Programme Management	**1.2 Programme management**	
12 Project (Environment) Context	**1.3 Portfolio management**	New topic – Portfolio Management split out of Programme Management
	1.4 Project context	Topic name changed
	1.5 Project sponsorship	New topic
	1.6 Project office	New topic
2 Strategic	*2 Planning the strategy*	Section name changed
20 Project Success Criteria	**2.1 Project success and benefits management**	Topic name changed – Benefits Management added
21 Strategy/Project Management Plan	**2.2 Stakeholder management**	New topic – previously covered within other topics
22 Value Management	2.3 Value management	

131

Fourth edition, 2000[a]	Fifth edition, 2006[b]	Comments
23 Risk Management	**2.4 Project management plan**	Topic name changed
24 Quality Management	**2.5 Project risk management**	Topic name changed
25 Health, Safety and Environment	**2.6 Project quality management**	Topic name changed
	2.7 Health, safety and environmental management	Topic name changed
3 Control	*3 Executing the strategy*	Section name changed
30 Work Content and Scope Management	**3.1 Scope management**	Topic name changed
31 Time Scheduling/Phasing	**3.2 Scheduling**	Topic name changed
32 Resource Management	**3.3 Resource management**	
33 Budgeting and Cost Management	3.4 Budgeting and cost management	
34 Change Control	**3.5 Change control**	
35 Earned Value Management	3.6 Earned value management	
36 Information Management	**3.7 Information management and reporting**	Topic name changed – Reporting added
	3.8 Issue management	New topic
4 Technical	*4 Techniques*	Section name changed
40 Design, Implementation and Handover Management	4.1 Requirements management	Topic moved
41 Requirements Management	4.2 Development	New topic
42 Estimating	**4.3 Estimating**	
43 Technology Management	4.4 Technology management	Emphasis of topic changed
44 Value Engineering	4.5 Value engineering	
45 Modelling and Testing	4.6 Modelling and testing	
46 Configuration Management	**4.7 Configuration management**	
5 Commercial	*5 Business and commercial*	Section name changed
50 Business Case	**5.1 Business case**	
51 Marketing and Sales	5.2 Marketing and sales	
52 Financial Management	5.3 Project financing and funding	Topic name changed

53 Procurement	**5.4 Procurement**	Section name changed
54 Legal Awareness	5.5 Legal awareness	
6 Organisational	*6 Organisation and governance*	Topic name changed
60 Life Cycle Design and Management	**6.1 Project life cycles**	
61 Opportunity	6.2 Concept	Topic name changed
62 Design and Development	6.3 Definition	Topic name changed
63 Implementation	6.4 Implementation	
64 Hand-Over	**6.5 Handover and closeout**	Topic name changed
65 (Post) Project Evaluation Review	**6.6 Project reviews**	Topic name changed
66 Organisation Structure	6.7 Organisation structure	
67 Organisational Roles	**6.8 Organisational roles**	
	6.9 Methods and procedures	New topic
	6.10 Governance of project management	New topic
7 People	*7 People and the profession*	Section name changed
70 Communication	**7.1 Communication**	
71 Teamwork	**7.2 Teamwork**	
72 Leadership	**7.3 Leadership**	
73 Conflict Management	7.4 Conflict management	
74 Negotiation	7.5 Negotiation	
75 Personnel Management	7.6 Human resource management	Topic name changed
	7.7 Behavioural characteristics	Transferred from 4th edition Preface
	7.8 Learning and development	New topic
	7.9 Professionalism and ethics	New topic

[a] Bold: topics included in Version 1 of the Introductory Certificate syllabus.
[b] Bold: topics included in Version 2 of the Introductory Certificate syllabus.

Appendix 4: Glossary of project management terms

Asterisks indicate definitions that are also published in BS 6079–2 : 2000. Permission to reproduce these extracts is granted by the BSI. British standards can be obtained from BSI customer services, 389 Chiswick High Road, London, W4 4AL; telephone: +44 (0)20 8996 9001.

This is a reduced selection of glossary terms and has been reproduced from the *APM Body of Knowledge 5th edition* with the permission of the Association for Project Management

Accept
A response to a risk (threat or opportunity) where no course of action is taken.

Acceptance
The formal process of accepting delivery of a deliverable or a product.

Acceptance criteria
The requirements and essential conditions that have to be achieved before project deliverables are accepted.

Acceptance test*
A formal, predefined test conducted to determine the compliance of the deliverable(s) with the acceptance criteria.

Activity*
A task, job, operation or process consuming time and possibly other resources. (The smallest self-contained unit of work used to define the logic of a project.)

Activity duration
The length of time that it takes to complete an activity.

Assumptions
Statements that will be taken for granted as fact and upon which the project business case will be justified.

Assurance
The process of examining with the intent to verify. *See* **quality assurance**.

Audit*
The systematic retrospective examination of the whole, or part, of a project or function to measure conformance to predetermined standards.

Avoid
A response to a threat that eliminates its probability or impact on the project.

Bar chart*
A chart on which activities and their durations are represented by lines drawn to a common timescale. *See* **Gantt chart**.

Baseline*
The reference levels against which the project is monitored and controlled.

Baseline plan
The fixed project plan. It is the standard by which performance against the project plan is measured.

Benefit
The quantifiable and measurable improvement resulting from completion of project deliverables that is perceived as positive

by a stakeholder. It will normally have a tangible value, expressed in monetary terms that will justify the investment.

Benefits management
The identification of the benefits (of a project or programme) at an organisational level and the tracking and realisation of those benefits.

Benefits realisation review
A review undertaken after a period of operations of the project deliverables. It is intended to establish that project benefits have been or are being realised.

Body of knowledge
An inclusive term that describes the sum of knowledge within the profession of project management. As with other professions, such as law and medicine, the body of knowledge rests with the practitioners and academics that apply and advance it.

Bottleneck
A process constraint that determines the capacity or capability of a system and restricts the rate, volume or flow of a process.

Bottom-up estimating
An estimating technique based on making estimates for every work package (or activity) in the work breakdown structure and summarising them to provide a total estimate of cost or effort required.

Breakdown structure
A hierarchical structure by which project elements are broken down, or decomposed. *See* **cost breakdown structure (CBS)**, **organisational breakdown structure (OBS)**, **product breakdown structure (PBS)**, **risk breakdown structure (RBS)** and **work breakdown structure (WBS)**.

Budget*
The agreed cost of the project or a quantification of resources needed to achieve an activity by a set time, within

which the activity owners are required to work.

Business-as-usual
An organisation's normal day-to-day operations.

Business case
The justification for undertaking a project, in terms of evaluating the benefit, cost and risk of alternative options and the rationale for the preferred solution. Its purpose is to obtain management commitment and approval for investment in the project. The business case is owned by the sponsor.

Change
A change to a project's baseline scope, cost, time or quality objectives.

Change control
A process that ensures that all changes made to a project's baseline scope, cost, time or quality objectives are identified, evaluated, approved, rejected or deferred.

Change control board
A formally constituted group of stakeholders responsible for approving or rejecting changes to the project baselines.

Change log
A record of all project changes, proposed, authorised, rejected or deferred.

Change management
The formal process through which changes to the project plan are approved and introduced. Also the process by which organisational change is introduced.

Change request
A request to obtain formal approval for changes to the scope, design, methods, costs or planned aspects of a project.

Client
The party to a contract who commissions work and pays for it on completion.

Closeout

The process of finalising all project matters, carrying out final project reviews, archiving project information and redeploying the remaining project team. *See* **handover and closeout**.

Communication

The giving, receiving, processing and interpretation of information. Information can be conveyed verbally, non-verbally, actively, passively, formally, informally, consciously or unconsciously.

Communication plan

A document that identifies what information is to be communicated to whom, why, when, where, how and through which medium, and the desired impact.

Communication planning

The establishment of project stakeholders' communication and information needs.

Comparative estimating

An estimating technique based on the comparison with, and factoring from, the cost of a previous similar project or operation.

Concept (phase)

The first phase in the project life cycle. During the concept phase the need, opportunity or problem is confirmed, the overall feasibility of the project is considered and a preferred solution identified.

Configuration*

Functional and physical characteristics of a deliverable (product) as defined in technical documents and achieved in the product.

Configuration audit

A check to ensure that all deliverables (products) in a project conform with one another and to the current specification. It ensures that relevant quality assurance procedures have been implemented and that there is consistency throughout project documentation.

Configuration control

A system to ensure that all changes to configuration items are controlled. An important aspect is being able to identify the interrelationships between configuration items.

Configuration identification

The unique identification of all items within the configuration. It involves breaking down the project into component parts or configuration items and creating a unique numbering or referencing system for each item and establishing configuration baselines.

Configuration item

A part of a configuration that has a set function and is designated for configuration management. It identifies uniquely all items within the configuration.

Configuration management*

Technical and administrative activities concerned with the creation, maintenance and controlled change of configuration throughout the project or product life cycle. See BS EN ISO 10007 for guidance on configuration management, including specialist terminology.

Constraints

Things that should be considered as fixed or must happen. Restrictions that will affect the project.

Continuous improvement

A business philosophy popularised in Japan where it is known as kaizen. Continuous improvement creates steady growth and improvement by keeping a business focused on its goals and priorities. It is a planned systematic approach to improvement on a continual basis.

Cost–benefit analysis*

An analysis of the relationship between the costs of undertaking an activity or project, initial and recurrent, and the benefits likely to arise from the changed situation, initially and recurrently.

Cost breakdown structure* (CBS)
The hierarchical breakdown of a project into cost elements.

Critical activity
An activity is termed critical when it has zero or negative float. Alternatively, an activity that has the lowest float on the project.

Critical path*
A sequence of activities through a project network from start to finish, the sum of whose durations determines the overall project duration. There may be more than one such path. The path through a series of activities, taking into account interdependencies, in which the late completion of activities will have an impact on the project end date or delay a key milestone.

Critical success factor
See **success factors**.

Definition (phase)
The second phase of the project life cycle. During the definition phase the preferred solution is further evaluated and optimised. Often an iterative process, definition can affect requirements and the project's scope, time, cost and quality objectives.

Deliverables*
The end products of a project or the measurable results of intermediate activities within the project organisation. *See* **product**.

Dependencies*
Something on which successful delivery of the project critically depends, which may often be outside the sphere of influence of the project manager, for example another project. Alternatively, dependency, a precedence relationship: a restriction that means that one activity has to precede, either in part or in total, another activity.

Duration
The length of time needed to complete the project or an activity.

Effectiveness
A measure of how well an action meets its intended requirements.

Enhance
A response to an opportunity that increases its probability, impact or both on the project.

Environment
The project environment is the context within which the project is formulated, assessed and realised. This includes all external factors that have an impact on the project.

Escalation
The process by which aspects of the project such as issues are drawn to the attention of those senior to the project manager, such as the sponsor, steering group or project board.

Estimate
An approximation of project time and cost targets, refined throughout the project life cycle.

Estimating
The use of a range of tools and techniques to produce estimates.

Exception report*
A focused report drawing attention to instances where planned and actual results are expected to be, or are already, significantly different.

Exploit
A response to an opportunity that maximises both its probability and impact on the project.

External environment
The environment in which the project must be undertaken that is external to the organisation carrying out the project.

Fitness for purpose
The degree to which the project management process and project deliverables satisfy stakeholder needs. *See* **quality**.

Float
See **free float** and **total float**.

Free float*
Time by which an activity may be delayed or extended without affecting the start of any succeeding activity.

Gantt chart*
A particular type of bar chart used in project management showing planned activity against time. A Gantt chart is a time-phased graphic display of activity durations. Activities are listed with other tabular information on the left-hand side, with time intervals over the bars. Activity durations are shown in the form of horizontal bars.

Gate review
A formal point in a project where its expected worth, progress, cost and execution plan are reviewed and a decision is made whether to continue with the next phase or stage of the project.

Handover
The point in the life cycle where deliverables are handed over to the sponsor and users. *See* **handover and closeout**.

Handover and closeout (phase)
The fourth and final phase in the project life cycle. During this phase final project deliverables are handed over to the sponsor and users. Closeout is the process of finalising all project matters, carrying out final project reviews, archiving project information and redeploying the project team.

Histogram
A graphic display of planned and/or actual resource usage over a period of time. It is in the form of a vertical bar chart, the height of each bar representing the quantity of resource usage in a given time unit. Bars may be single or multiple, or show stacked resources.

Impact
The assessment of the effect on an objective of a risk occurring.

Implementation (phase)
The third phase of the project life cycle where the project management plan (PMP) is executed, monitored and controlled. During this phase the design is finalised and used to build the deliverables.

Internal environment
The environment in which the project must be undertaken that is internal to the organisation carrying out the project.

Issue
A threat to the project objectives that cannot be resolved by the project manager.

Issue log
A log of all issues raised during a project or programme, showing details of each issue, its evaluation, what decisions were made and its current status.

Issue management
The process by which concerns that threaten the project objectives and cannot be resolved by the project manager can be identified and addressed to remove the threats that they pose.

Key events
Major events, the achievement of which is deemed to be critical to the execution of the project.

Key performance indicators (KPIs)
Measures of success that can be used throughout the project to ensure that it is progressing towards a successful conclusion.

Leadership
The ability to establish vision and direction, to influence and align others towards a

common purpose, and to empower and inspire people to achieve project success. It enables the project to proceed in an environment of change and uncertainty.

Life cycle
See **project life cycles**.

Life cycle cost
The cumulative cost of a project over its whole life cycle.

Make or buy decision
The decision to make a deliverable internally or to buy a finished deliverable from a supplier, for example, develop a software application in house or purchase an existing application.

Milestone*
A key event. An event selected for its importance in the project.

Milestone plan
A plan containing milestones that highlight key points of the project.

Monitoring
The recording, analysing and reporting of project performance as compared to the plan in order to identify and report deviations.

Need, problem or opportunity
The underlying reason for undertaking a project. Without a definable need, problem or opportunity a project should not go ahead.

Network diagram
A pictorial presentation of project data in which the project logic is the main determinant of the placement of the activities in the drawing. Frequently called a flowchart, PERT chart, logic drawing, activity network or logic diagram.

Objectives
Predetermined results towards which effort is directed.

Opportunity
A positive risk; a risk that if it occurs will have a beneficial effect on the project. A positive aspect of project uncertainty, it may also help to negate threats.

Organisational breakdown structure (OBS)*
A hierarchical way in which the organisation may be divided into management levels and groups, for planning and control purposes.

Organisational roles
The roles performed by individuals or groups in a project. Both roles and responsibilities within projects must be defined to address the transient and unique nature of projects, and to ensure that clear accountabilities can be assigned.

Outputs
Deliverables that are the result of a process. *See* **deliverables**.

Parametric estimating
An estimating technique that uses a statistical relationship between historic data and other variables (for example, square metreage in construction, lines of code in software development) to calculate an estimate.

Performance
The quality of the delivery and the deliverables (outputs) of the project.

Phase (of a project)*
Part of a project during which a set of related and interlinked activities are performed to attain a designated objective. One of a series of distinct steps in carrying out a project that together constitute the project life cycle.

Phase review
A review that takes place at the end of a life cycle phase. *See* **gate review**.

Planning
The process of identifying the means, resources and actions necessary to accomplish an objective.

Portfolio

A grouping of an organisation's projects, programmes and related business-as-usual activities, taking into account resource constraints. Portfolios can be managed at an organisational, programme or functional level.

Portfolio management

The selection and management of all of an organisation's projects, programmes and related operational activities, taking into account resource constraints.

Post-project review

A review undertaken after the project deliverables have been handed over and before final closeout, intended to produce lessons learnt that will enable continuous improvement.

Precedence network*

A multiple dependency network. An activity-on-node network in which a sequence arrow represents one of four forms of precedence relationship, depending on the positioning of the head and the tail of the sequence arrow. The relationships are:

● **finish to start**
start of activity depends on finish of preceding activity, either immediately or after a lapse of time;

● **finish to finish**
finish of activity depends on finish of preceding activity, either immediately or after a lapse of time;

● **start to start**
start of activity depends on start of preceding activity, either immediately or after a lapse of time;

● **start to finish**
finish of activity depends on start of preceding activity, either immediately or after a lapse of time).

Predecessor

An activity that must be completed (or be partially completed) before a specified activity can begin.

Probability

The likelihood of a risk occurring.

Problem

In project management terms, a concern that the project manager has to deal with on a day-to-day basis.

Process*

A set of interrelated resources and activities that transform inputs into outputs.

Procurement

The process by which the resources (goods and services) required by a project are acquired. It includes development of the procurement strategy, preparation of contracts, selection and acquisition of suppliers, and management of the contracts.

Procurement strategy

A strategy that sets out how to acquire and manage resources (goods and services) required by a project.

Product

See **deliverables**.

Product breakdown structure (PBS)

A hierarchy of deliverables that are required to be produced on the project. This forms the base document from which the execution strategy and product-based work breakdown structure may be derived. It provides a guide for configuration control documentation.

Programme

A group of related projects, which may include related business-as-usual activities that together achieve a beneficial change of a strategic nature for an organisation.

Programme management

The coordinated management of related projects, which may include related business-as-usual activities, that together achieve a beneficial change of a strategic nature for an organisation.

Programme manager
The individual with responsibility for managing a programme.

Progress
The partial completion of a project, or a measure of the same.

Progress report
A regular report to senior personnel, sponsors or stakeholders summarising the progress of a project including key events, milestones, costs and other issues.

Project
A unique, transient endeavour undertaken to achieve a desired outcome.

Project board
See **steering group**.

Project context
The environment within which a project is undertaken. Projects do not exist in a vacuum and an appreciation of the context within which the project is being performed will assist those involved in project management to deliver a project.

Project evaluation review
A documented review of the project's performance, produced at predefined points in the project life cycle.

Project life cycles
All projects follow a life cycle and life cycles will differ across industries and business sectors. A life cycle allows the project to be considered as a sequence of distinct phases (concept, definition, implementation, and handover and closeout) that provide the structure and approach for progressively delivering the required outputs.

Project management
The process by which projects are defined, planned, monitored, controlled and delivered so that agreed benefits are realised.

Project management plan (PMP)
A plan that brings together all the plans for a project. The purpose of the PMP is to document the outcome of the planning process and to provide the reference document for managing the project. The PMP is owned by the project manager.

Project management processes
The generic processes that need to apply to each phase of the project life cycle. These may be described as a starting or initiating process, a defining and planning process, a monitoring and controlling process, and a learning or closing process.

Project management team
Members of the project team who are directly involved in its management.

Project manager*
The individual responsible and accountable for the successful delivery of the project.

Project objectives
Those things that are to be achieved by the project, which usually include technical, time, cost and quality objectives but may include other items to meet stakeholder needs.

Project quality management
The discipline that is applied to ensure that both the outputs of the project and the processes by which the outputs are delivered meet the required needs of stakeholders. Quality is broadly defined as fitness for purpose or more narrowly as the degree of conformance of the outputs and process.

Project risk
The exposure of stakeholders to the consequences of variation in outcome.

Project risk management
A structured process that allows individual risk events and overall project risk to be understood and managed

proactively, optimising project success by minimising threats and maximising opportunities.

Project roles and responsibilities
The roles and responsibilities of those involved in the project, for example, the sponsor and project manager.

Project schedule*
The timetable for a project. It shows how project activities and milestones are planned over a period of time. It is often shown as a milestone chart, Gantt or other bar chart, or as a tabular listing of dates.

Project sponsor
See **sponsor**.

Project sponsorship
An active senior management role, responsible for identifying the business need, problem or opportunity. The sponsor ensures the project remains a viable proposition and that benefits are realised, resolving any issues outside the control of the project manager.

Project status report
A report on the status of accomplishments and any variances to spending and schedule plans.

Project steering group
See **steering group**.

Project success
The satisfaction of stakeholder needs measured by the success criteria as identified and agreed at the start of the project.

Project success criteria
See **success criteria**.

Project team
A set of individuals, groups and/or organisations responsible to the project manager for working towards a common purpose.

Quality
The fitness for purpose or the degree of conformance of the outputs of the process.

Quality assurance (QA)
The process of evaluating overall project performance on a regular basis to provide confidence that the project will satisfy the relevant quality standards.

Quality audit
An official examination to determine whether practices conform to specified standards, or a critical analysis of whether a deliverable meets quality criteria.

Quality control (QC)
The process of monitoring specific project results to determine if they comply with relevant standards, and identifying ways to eliminate causes of unsatisfactory performance.

Quality plan (for a project)*
That part of the project plan that concerns quality management and quality assurance strategies (see also ISO 10006).

Quality planning
The process of determining which quality standards are necessary and how to apply them.

Reduce
A response to a threat that reduces its probability, impact or both on the project.

Reporting
Taking information and presenting it in an appropriate format which includes the formal communication of project information to stakeholders.

Report
The presentation of information in an appropriate format. Alternatively, a written record or summary, a detailed account or statement or a verbal account.

Requirements
A statement of the need that a project has to satisfy. It should be comprehensive, clear, well structured, traceable and testable.

Resource levelling
Resource levelling can be applied to projects when there are resource constraints. Resource levelling forces the amount of work scheduled not to exceed the limits of resources available. This results in either activity durations being extended or entire activities being delayed to periods when resources are available. This often results in a longer project duration. It is also known as resource-limited scheduling.

Resource-limited scheduling
See **resource levelling**.

Resource management
A process that identifies and assigns resources to activities so that the project is undertaken using appropriate levels of resources and within an acceptable duration.

Resource smoothing*
A process applied to projects to ensure that resources are used as efficiently as possible. It involves utilising float within the project or increasing or decreasing the resources required for specific activities, such that any peaks and troughs of resource usage are smoothed out. This does not affect the project duration. It is also known as time-limited scheduling.

Resources
All those items required to undertake a project, including people, finance and materials.

Responsibility assignment matrix (RAM)
A diagram or chart showing assigned responsibilities for elements of work. It is created by combining the work breakdown structure with the organisational breakdown structure.

Rework
Repeating work already completed in producing a deliverable in order to remove defects and meet acceptance criteria.

Risk*
See **project risk** and **risk event**.

Risk assessment
The process of quantifying the likelihood of risks occurring and assessing their likely impact on the project.

Risk breakdown structure (RBS)
A hierarchical breakdown of the risks on a project.

Risk event
An uncertain event or set of circumstances that if realised would have an effect on the achievement of one or more of the project objectives.

Risk identification*
The process of identifying project risks.

Risk log
A document that provides identification, estimation, impact evaluation and countermeasures for all risks to the project. It is normally maintained throughout the life of the project.

Risk owner
The person who has responsibility for dealing with a particular risk on a project and for identifying and managing responses.

Risk response
An action or set of actions to reduce the probability or impact of a threat or to increase the probability or impact of an opportunity.

Risk response planning
The planning of responses to risks.

Schedule
The timetable for a project. It shows how project activities and milestones are planned over a period of time. It is often shown as a milestone chart, Gantt or other bar chart, or as a tabular listing of dates.

Scheduling
The process used to determine the overall project duration. This includes identification of activities and their

logical dependencies, and estimating activity durations, taking into account requirements and availability of resources.

Scope

The sum of work content of a project.

Scope creep

The term sometimes given to the continual extension of the scope of some projects.

Scope management

The process by which the deliverables and the work to produce these are identified and defined. Identification and definition of the scope must describe what the project will include and what it will not include, i.e. what is in and out of scope.

Share

A response to an opportunity that increases its probability, impact or both on the project by sharing the risk with a third party.

Slack

An alternative term for float. *See* **free float** and **total float**.

Sponsor

The individual or body for whom the project is undertaken and who is the primary risk-taker. The sponsor owns the business case and is ultimately responsible for the project and for delivering the benefits.

Stage

A subdivision of the life cycle phase into a natural subsection with well-defined deliverables.

Stakeholder

The organisations or people who have an interest or role in the project or are impacted by the project.

Stakeholder analysis

The identification of stakeholder groups, their interest levels and ability to influence the project or programme.

Stakeholder identification

The process of identifying stakeholders in a project.

Stakeholder management

The systematic identification, analysis and planning of actions to communicate with, negotiate with and influence stakeholders.

Status report

A description of where the project currently stands, usually in the form of a written report, issued to both the project team and other responsible people on a regular basis, stating the status of an activity, work package or whole project. It may be a formal report on the input, issues and actions resulting from a status meeting.

Steering group

A group, usually comprising the sponsor, senior managers and sometimes key stakeholders, whose remit is to set the strategic direction of a project. It gives guidance to the sponsor and project manager. Often referred to as the project board.

Success criteria

The qualitative or quantitative measures by which the success of the project is judged.

Success factors

Factors that when present in the project environment are most conducive to the achievement of a successful project. The success factors that if absent would cause the project to fail are sometimes termed critical success factors (CSFs).

Successor

An activity whose start or finish depends on the start or finish of a predecessor activity.

Supplier

A contractor, consultant or any organisation that supplies resources to the project.

Task

The smallest indivisible part of an activity when it is broken down to a level best understood and performed by a specific person or organisation.

Team building

The ability to gather the right people to join a project team and get them working together for the benefit of a project

Team development

The process of developing skills, as a group and individually, that enhance project performance

Team member

A person who is accountable to and has work assigned to them by the project manager to be performed either by them or by others in a working group.

Teamwork

The process whereby people work collaboratively towards a common goal, as distinct from other ways that individuals can work within a group.

Threat

A negative risk; a risk that if it occurs will have a detrimental effect on the project.

Time-limited scheduling*
See **resource smoothing**.

Total float*

Time by which an activity may be delayed or extended without affecting the total project duration or violating a target finish date.

Transfer

A response to a threat that reduces its probability, impact on the project or both by transferring the risk to a third party.

Uncertainty

A state of incomplete knowledge about a proposition. Usually associated with risks, both threats and opportunities.

User requirements

The requirements governing the project's deliverables or products as expressed by the user. What the user needs expressed in user terminology.

Users

The group of people who are intended to benefit from the project or operate the deliverables.

Version control

The recording and management of the configuration of different versions of the project's products.

Work breakdown structure* (WBS)

A way in which a project may be divided by level into discrete groups for programming, cost planning and control purposes. The WBS is a tool for defining the hierarchical breakdown of work required to deliver the products of a project. Major categories are broken down into smaller components. These are subdivided until the lowest required level of detail is established. The lowest units of the WBS are generally work packages. In some instances work packages are further divided into activities that become the activities in a project. The WBS defines the total work to be undertaken on the project and provides a structure for all project control systems.

Work package*

A group of related activities that are defined at the same level within a work breakdown structure.

Index

Entries in bold and italic refer to definitions of terms.

NOTES

NOTES

NOTES

NOTES

NOTES

NOTES

NOTES

NOTES